THE SPIRIT JOURNEY

MADI KERTONEGORO

THE
SPIRIT
JOURNEY

Stories and Paintings of Bali

Introduction by Alice Walker

WILD TREES PRESS

Published by
WILD TREES PRESS
P.O. Box 378
Navarro, California 95463

Copyright © 1988 by Wild Trees Press

ISBN 0-931125-06-5
Library of Congress Catalog Card: 87-51617
Edited by Stephanie T. Fried
Translated by Judy Marentetee and Madi Kertonegoro
Originally published by the Harkat Foundation, Bali, Indonesia, 1986

Cover painting: "Affandi, the son of nature/*Affandi si anak alam*"
by Madi Kertonegoro. Oil on canvas, 1986, 80 × 100 cm.
Book and cover design by Nancy Austin
Lontar palm leaf illustrations by I Wayan Suweca
Composition by Designer Type

Printed and bound by Bookcrafters
Chelsea, Michigan

10 9 8 7 6 5 4 3 2 1

To my mother,
Sudarti Sofyant Hadi Sarono,
Who always told me I wasn't crazy.

Contents

Acknowledgements

Thank you to Mangku Widia, Kondri, Salin, and the other villagers of Tenganan who shared their stories with me; to I Nyoman Sadra, the Chief of Tenganan, for his advice and assistance;
     To Gusti Ngurah Geridig and the people of Bedahulu for their stories; to I Wayan Suweca, Tenganan, for translating *The Spirit Journey* into **lontar** illustrations; to the Archeological Museum, Bedahulu, for permitting me access to its archives;
     To Inez Baranay, Australia, and Gde Aryantha Soethama, Denpasar, for advice and assistance; to Agung Wiryawan, Amlapura, for his support; to Alice Walker and Robert Allen, USA, for encouraging me to write; to Tressa Kosaki, Kathryn Gardiner, Bette Brandon, Australia, and Lynne and Anoy Dean, New Zealand, for a fine job of typing;
     To Masahiko Yasuda, Japan, for help with transportation; and to Komang Sudana and his family, Homestay Kelapa Mas, Candi Dasa, for their smiles, their coffee, and for letting me sleep on their floor.

MADI KERTONEGORO

Foreword

The island of Bali, like the rest of Indonesia, is extremely rich in oral folklore. Each district has its own stories and origin mythologies.

The village of Tenganan, where Madi collected the stories that make up *The Spirit Journey,* is inhabited by people who are thought to be some of the "original Balinese," or Bali Aga. Many of the Tenganan traditions and ceremonies are found nowhere else on the island. The villagers are renowned for weaving the exquisite **kain gringsing,** or "flaming cloth" using the complex double **ikat** process. Once a year, a contest of strength and endurance for young men, the Pandan war, is held during the month-long Usaba Sambah ceremony.

Traditionally, the legends and literature of Tenganan village were inscribed on **lontar** palm leaves and stored in the library pavillion. In 1841, the pavillion burned down and most of the village **lontars** were destroyed.

With *The Spirit Journey,* Madi has begun the valuable work of collecting and recording some of the lost legends of Tenganan village.

STEPHANIE T. FRIED
Tenganan, Bali, 1986

About This Book

When I arrived in Candi Dasa village in Bali (March, 1986) I was intrigued by a written notice asking for help in turning a local oral history into "good English." That is how I met Madi Kertonegoro, a Javanese-born artist who has lived in Bali for over a decade. I read his earlier books, *The Man From Behind the Mist* and *Voice of the Eyes* and willingly joined the team which helped Madi produce *The Spirit Journey.*

Madi and Judy Marentetee, a Canadian, worked together on the translation—Madi reading his Indonesian script aloud sentence by sentence in rough English, referring to the dictionary when he needed to explain a particular word or phrase.

The editor, Stephanie Fried, an American, was coaxed away from her research on Balinese agriculture long enough to help organize the book.

Typing was done by various visitors who turned up and undertook a few days' work, sometimes in exchange for food or meals.

The book was put together in the informal way that things get done in Bali. They get done most easily when a Westerner's "logical" and "ordered" approach is not used.

The translator and editor have corrected only the most glaring transgressions of the basic rules of English, those that would hinder legibility. Otherwise the "translated flavor" has been preserved. It is deliberate. The contents of the narrative and the thought that informs it are distinctly un-English, and to the foreign reader that is, I believe, part of the charm of this work.

The narrative itself, the stories-within-stories, prove that story-telling is a universal art.

The reader, whether in Bali or abroad, who shares the world of *The Spirit Journey* will experience sharp and comic observations of life in present-day Bali, with its tourists and new ecological challenges, woven in with old tales of mystery and imagination.

INEZ BARANAY
April 1986

Introduction

One rainy February day in 1986 my companion Robert Allen and my daughter Rebecca Walker and I savored a leisurely lunch at a small restaurant called Murni's at the end of the main road of Ubud, Bali. Murni's was just down the hill from our rented house and we enjoyed eating there; the food was tasty, the waitresses courteous, the view from the back windows charming—and, best of all, on a rack in the middle of the floor there were newspapers and magazines from all over the lower half of the world: Indonesia, New Zealand, Australia, Fiji, etc., and books!

Our habit was to saunter into the restaurant around one in the afternoon and, between eating and reading, stay until about three. It was in Murni's that I noticed the compelling face of a man looking down at me from the cover of a small book. I took it from the rack and brought it to our table. It was called *Voice of the Eyes* by someone named Madi Kertonegoro. I noticed that the man's ears were very large, and stuck out from his head like flaps, but it was his eyes that both listened and spoke. So much pain, I read in his eyes, and wisdom and compassion too. He was also dressed oddly, half Balinese, half Charles Lindbergh. In fact, he had the aspect of an earthling who has somehow managed a sojourn in outer space, looked down on all our planetary confusion from that enlightening height, and then returned out of pity and empathy for us all. You're a mess, his eyes said, but how I love you.

That night I read *Voice of the Eyes*, liked it very much, and passed it on to Robert. This is wonderful! he exclaimed. We must find the author and see if he will let us publish his stories—and I hope he has more of them—in America! There's so little on Bali to read at home, he continued, and none of the folkstories that really help you know who people are.

So off we went next day in search of Madi Kertonegoro. Luckily *Voice of the Eyes* had the address of his gallery written on the cover. We asked directions ("Sure, go straight until you come to where that big tree used to be, then turn right and then . . .") and soon arrived on his doorstep. We introduced ourselves to Madi Kertonegoro, a beautiful, slender, longhaired brownskin man who was born in Java but has lived in Bali for over ten years. He was quiet and thoughtful, very much aware of world events and politics, and given to subtle joking. His "Future Peace Art Gallery" sign bore a hand-drawn peace symbol. "Here is my work," he said, escorting us into his small gallery. It is only the truth to say that we were not only moved by what we saw, but astonished. For we had come to talk with a folklorist and storyteller, someone who cared enough about the people of Bali to collect and save their "race memories." But what we'd also found was a great painter.

In Bali, of course, everyone paints. After the rice is harvested and the long rainy season sets in, painting, sculpting, making music and fine cloths and dancing and making exquisite offerings to the gods seems all that the people do. And I agree with all my heart that it's enough. But Madi's paintings, given his Dutch-influenced Javanese background, perhaps, were unlike any of the painting

xiv

we'd seen in Bali, and by that time we'd seen a lot. Where the classical Balinese painting relies heavily on traditional and non-specific subjects—so that one sees endless rice paddies and waterfalls and beautiful brown people gathering the harvest, Madi's paintings showed real people. His brother, his grandmother (my favorite of all his paintings), his friends, old men he obviously spent time talking with, listening to, and loved; in short, people that one felt he knew. And as in all the best "realistic" art, Madi's paintings also captured spirit.

Nor was he, again unlike many of the painters whose work we saw in Ubud, painting for the tourists. Several of his paintings were priced casually in the thousands of dollars. The one of his grandmother and others were tagged "not for sale." Yet Madi lived very modestly, in the Balinese fashion: a small room for sleeping, with a tiny porch for entertaining guests, and another small room separate, for cooking. And the gallery. He spoke of his efforts to make ends meet, joking about the scrawny chicken he'd found that day in the market and that he invited us back that night to share. It was clear both that he treasured the people who were his subjects, and that he valued his own work.

Wild Trees Press is happy to publish *The Spirit Journey; Stories and Paintings of Bali*. It is our hope that it will serve to help bring the people of our country, the United States of North America, closer to the people of Bali, Indonesia, a people whose cultural integrity, personal gentleness and courtesy, and collective spirituality was a much appreciated gift to three "spirit journeyers" during those rainy February days of not so long ago.

ALICE WALKER
Wild Trees
Mendocino County, California
October 7, 1987

PAINTINGS BY
MADI KERTONEGORO

with accompanying text by the artist

Visitor from above the wind

One day in the stifling heat, a spaceship parked on top of the clouds. The passenger descended to earth in the rice field, just to the north of my house. His ears were very large. His body and clothes were exactly like a Balinese.

After bowing politely, that being spoke in a language I didn't understand. However, by using spiritual power, I was able to communicate with him. He was thirsty.

I took a glass of water. He drank, guzzling it down quickly. And then nodded, ready to leave.

"Why are your ears so large; and why do you carry that coconut in your hand?" I asked spontaneously.

According to him, his large ears made him more sensitive to natural and social phenomena. The coconut was a sacred talisman or gathering place of the spirits to scare away corruption, because corrupt people would be afraid of the power of the talisman from the country above the wind.

Once again he nodded, and then with a long cry he leapt up into his vehicle.

Cessttt .... in one second the spaceship disappeared from my eyes, splitting the sky.

Suddenly, before I realized, seven coconut trees fell down, burning, to the ground.

I was surprised. This was not a dream!!

Visitor from above the wind/*Pendatang dari atas angin*.
Oil on canvas, 1985, 90 × 145 cm.

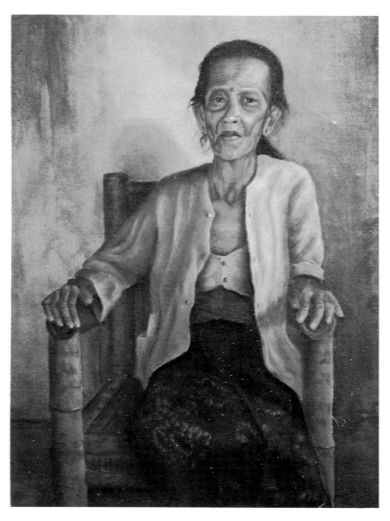

My grandmother "Soerip Martoyatiman"/
Nenekku "Soerip Martoyatiman."
Oil on canvas, 1981, 80 × 100 cm.

The old Balinese kitchen/*Dapur tua di Bali.*
Oil on canvas, 1981, 55 × 65 cm.

Madi Kertonegoro and his Spirit of 1945/*Semangat '45.*
Oil on canvas, 1985, 50 × 60 cm.

My Young Brother, Ahmad Ashar/*Ahmad Ashar adikku*.
Oil on canvas, 1984, 50 × 60 cm.

Money changer/*Penukaran uang*.
Oil on canvas, 1987, 125 × 140 cm.

Happy carrying granddaughters/
Berbahagia menggendong dua cucunya.
Oil on canvas, 1987, 100 × 145 cm.

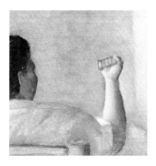

Uses of the rubber stamp

In modern times, as in colonial times, a person's destiny is determined by that capricious god, the rubber stamp!

It is the stamp that determines your fate. The wrong stamp may lead to the wrong fate. If the stamp says you are blacklisted, so be it, you are blacklisted. If the stamp says you are a good person, so be it, you are known as a good person.

The rubber stamp usually sleeps in the desk drawer. Sometimes, in the cold season, I have known stamps to ask for a blanket of money to ease their sleep. Have you known stamps like this?

So, if you are a polite person you must show great respect for Mr. Stamp. Long live Mr. Rubber Stamp!

The Stamp/*Stempel*.
Oil on canvas, 1984, 140 × 200 cm.

Waiting for the fruit of the trees of Industry/
Menanti buah pohon industri.
Oil on canvas, 1984, 145 × 275 cm.

Sadu's view of the world during nuclear war/
Dunia dalam pandangan Sang Sadu ketika perang nuklir.
Oil on canvas, 1985, 150 × 300 cm.

Messenger

One night, I was sitting outside my studio in the rice field, watching the soft light of the moon play over the young rice. Suddenly, everything became dark. A shadow had fallen between me and the moon. I was afraid and sought the safety of my studio which was brightly lit by a kerosene lamp. Usually my young brother could be found studying there at night, but this time the studio was empty. I was alone.

The shadow which had startled me so, followed me and waited politely outside the studio door. Ashamed at my lack of courtesy, I said to him "*Silahkan masuk,* please come in."

He came in and stood silhouetted against the wall, so that I could see him. In a soft voice he said, "You must share this letter with the inhabitants of your world; people of all nations, races, and beliefs." And his shadow hand reached forward and pressed the letter in my direction.

I asked if I could paint him. He agreed. Night after night, he came to visit me, always slipping away before dawn, until the painting was finished.

Once I asked him why he carried a newspaper in the pocket of his rumpled brown coat.

"Where I come from," he said thoughtfully, "we have a habit of collecting newspapers. We collect them from different cities, countries, and worlds. Recently, the newspapers from your world have been full of news about nuclear weapons, plans for nuclear war, and about an arms race between rival kingdoms. I read these things and could not stay away. I have seen this happen before. In my experience no one ever wins this kind of race."

"And the flashlight?" I asked. "Of what use is a flashlight to one like you?"

"Oh, this," he said, "This is a special light. I use it to light my way as I travel through the dark places of the universe."

After many nights, I finished the painting. I had learned much from my shadow friend. He begged permission to leave, as if for a long time.

The next morning, my young brother found his crumpled old coat at the edge of the rice field. In vain, I searched for the letter but it was nowhere to be found. How could this be? This letter I was meant to share with people everywhere, with the leaders of all nations. I felt dejected.

Suddenly, I realized that the letter was not lost. There it was, on canvas, painted for all to see in the hand of the shadow-messenger, the messenger of peace.

The Messenger of Peace/*Duta perdamaian.*
Oil on canvas, 1984, 80 × 100 cm.

Looking for new hope after nuclear war/
Mencari harapan baru setelah perang nuklir.
Oil on canvas, 1984, 100 × 145 cm.

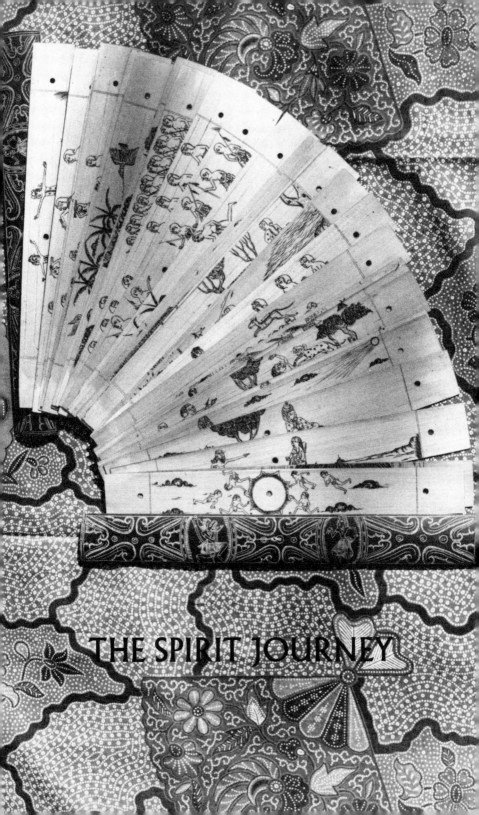

THE SPIRIT JOURNEY

I am a magical being, unseen by the eyes. Sometimes those with special powers can feel my presence. Spirit is my name.

I can go anywhere I want. I am not restricted by space. Not a secret in the world is a secret to me. All is open to me.

I can understand your secrets: how much money you are saving in the bank, how many lovers you have, what your thoughts are while you work, if you are honest or corrupt. I can know all, if I want.

Because I am Spirit, I cannot take a visible form. That is my weakness.

If I could change myself into a concrete object, surely that would cause a sensation in the world. For example, I could become the fruit on your table. When you or your guests picked up that fruit, I could change into smoke.

Or, maybe I would change myself into a bank with all of the valuables inside. While people are taking or leaving money, suddenly I would change myself into a discotheque and then disappear. Maybe I would reappear in the Campuan River and everyone would get wet.

Do not worry. All of that can never happen. As I

3

have already told you, I cannot change myself into a concrete object.

Sometimes, though, I can be very naughty.

One day I entered the heart of a man who was still drunk with love. I pushed him to come to his girlfriend's house in the darkness of the night. When he reached the front of her house, I was hanging and swaying in his heart, so without knocking on the door, he went in.

He saw his sweetheart hugging and kissing another man. The man whose heart I had entered became red in the face. I led him back home.

In his home, I blew the smoke of jealousy, so he could not sleep. In anguish, he decided to break up with his girlfriend.

What he didn't know was that the man who was hugging his sweetheart was actually her brother, who she had not seen in ten years. Of course, that was the result of my naughtiness.

I also do good things, too.

Once, I saw a rich person considering whether to buy a wood carving. He went into a big art shop. Soon I changed the voice of his heart so that he left the gallery. I encouraged him to take a walk to an isolated village, while I sang a Balinese gamelan melody.

I took him to I Kelincet, a poor wood carver in Petulu village. The rich man liked his carvings.

"Oh, we are lucky to meet," he said. "I'm not even sure why I came here." He gave many 10,000 Rupiah notes to the wood carver. I Kelincet's hands trembled as he received the money. Not long after that, I noticed I Kelincet and his younger brother in Denpasar at the secondhand bicycle market.

One Sunday, I saw a group of young children in Singaraja looking for fish with a basket in a stream. From morning until afternoon, not one fish did they catch. Maybe the fish were also on holiday.

4

I felt sorry for the children, so I entered the hand of the smallest boy. I pushed his hand into a hole underwater which was actually a place where fish were hiding. As the fish swam out, the children caught them in the basket.

How glad they were to catch so many fish! They ran home with their leaking plastic bag full of fish, laughing and shouting as the water made a trail behind them on the path.

Once, when I was passing over Candi Dasa beach, I looked down and saw two tourists wrestling, making love on the beach.

Earlier that day, the man had come from Penelokan, the woman from Denpasar. They met by accident on the bus which brought them together to Candi Dasa.

I know what country they came from, but there is no point in mentioning that. Let that become my secret.

It angered me to see that while the local villagers feel Candi Dasa to be a holy place, some visitors see the beauty of the beach from a different perspective.

I descended to earth, looking for a snake in the undergrowth. There was a zebra snake, yellow with black stripes—frightening, but not dangerous.

I brought the snake close to the two tourists and touched their faces. They turned pale. Together they screamed and ran away along the beach. They rushed into a homestay, out of breath.

I laughed. I was sure the villagers would have some questions the next morning; who owns the two pairs of underpants, red and blue? They will be even more astonished when they discover several condoms, still unused, scattered on the beach.

Now I am flying in the sky over Bali. It is almost nightfall and the electricity in Gianyar, Klungkung, Denpasar, and Singaraja lights up at almost the same moment. Ubud looks dark. There must be a problem with the electricity there.

In Peliatan, by the light of kerosene lamps, the Legong dancers are swaying on the stage while tourists look on, entranced.

Several hours later, all is quiet. Some visitors are still sitting and chatting in Ibu Jero Arsa's *warung*. She serves her customers' requests with friendliness. This she has done since before the tourists came to Bali. Several bats circle the nearby banyan tree in silence.

Far away to the east, in Candi Dasa, the fishing **prahus** search for fish in the middle of the sea. Their lamps look like fireflies. Some of the restaurants along the beach are still open. The waves are not so big, the weather is good. I can see the neighboring islands—Lombok, Nusa Penida, and Sumbawa, stretch away to the east.

To the south, more than ten motorbikes make the dust fly along Kuta Beach Road. The passengers are drunk and yelling wildly. Men and women are tightly packed in a big discotheque. They honey-talk each other.

I consider flying down, but I think it's better to watch from a distance.

Suddenly, from behind, an object as big as a grey whale rushes at me and, in fact, goes right through me. What a surprise! Oh, I see. It's just a Garuda plane going to Sydney. Good thing I am Spirit—I didn't feel a thing. The plane rocked back and forth and I heard an announcement from the pilot: "Sorry passengers, the plane is rocking because of weather problems." I just smile.

I no longer wish to look at the world from above so I enter a passing cloud. The wind pulls me and carries me until I feel cold and fall with the rain. I make myself smaller and enter a raindrop. I let myself fall onto the roof of a house. I roll to the ground, and stop against a bamboo wall. I ease quietly into a puddle.

Two people are talking. I move against the bamboo wall and peek in. Actually, it would have been easy for me to enter that room, but don't you think it's more enjoyable to peek and spy from outside?

Two people were talking seriously—a youth with shoulder-length hair and another, older man. Sometimes they whispered, sometimes they were angry, and after a while, I heard sighing. By then the rain had stopped; the neighbor's radio could no longer be heard. The old man sat in a bamboo chair. The boy sat beside him in a worn-out batik **sarong**. Each wore a small **kris** tucked into a **selendang** around his waist.

The roar of the waves in the distance was barely

7

audible. Bamboo trees brushed softly against each other. I continued peeping and listening to their conversation.

"I've been watching you for the past few days. You're quieter than usual. There are deep lines in your forehead. Please tell me. I can help you," said the old man.

The youth was as quiet as a statue. After a while, he stretched his legs. The bamboo chair creaked. He breathed deeply. His head dropped.

"Five days ago I went to the beach with some friends," he said. He swallowed and continued. "It was not like the years before. This year we only caught a few fish."

"Isn't this a good season for fishing?" asked the old man. "There is some rain, but the wind is not so fast. The weather isn't so cold."

"It is like that, Father, but there are really very few fish along the beach."

"And you felt disappointed?"

"Yes, Father." He looked up for a moment, then down again. "We brought many rods and hooks, and lots of hope."

"And you feel the world is no longer beautiful?"

"That's right, Father. The world seems no longer complete."

They stopped talking when they heard a sound, "krosok" from behind the house.

"Oh, that must be a coconut, fallen from the tree. Tomorrow we can look for it." The father shifted. The chair creaked. The youth nodded his head.

"The world seems empty, sucked dry, burned."

"Yes, sometimes it is difficult to see the beauty of the world," the old man said thoughtfully.

"But Father, all I want is to see the beauty!"

"Everybody wants it, but the non-beautiful is reality too! You must do something to make the ugly beautiful. The beauty which you dream of is not reality. It will only make you spoiled, frustrated, and weak," was the old man's stern reply.

"What do you mean, Father?"

"False beauty can capture you; you become afraid to see reality. You become dependent on it. That false beauty will frustrate you, and in the long run you become weak!" the father explained.

"Weak?"

"Yes, bewitched by false beauty, you become too lazy to move!"

A mosquito landed on the old man's leg. He slapped it with the palm of his right hand and the mosquito died. A spot of blood appeared on his skin; it must have already sucked his blood.

They were quiet for a few minutes. The wind entered through the bamboo wall and made the kerosene lamp flicker. They heard the "krosok" of another falling coconut.

"Can you understand what I mean?" the father began again.

"Yes, Father, but after that fishing incident, I feel fear. I feel as if the ocean is cursing humanity. The ocean is no longer generous," the son said haltingly.

"The ocean never curses. The ocean is never miserly! Human beings do not understand the ways of nature!" the old man exclaimed, coughing a little. "Men steal the goods of the ocean!"

"Ah, people do not steal from the ocean. The ocean gives willingly to man," the son argued.

"As long as the ocean is able to give, she will. Nature is fair. Only when she cannot give, she will not give," said the father, his forehead creasing.

The youth looked thoughtful, and pushed aside some of the hair that had fallen across his face.

"Nature has a law," the old man continued. "The ocean is part of nature. Many people steal coral from the ocean and bring it to the land. On the land, they burn it and process it for lime. The lime is used to build houses or hotels or streets."

"I know what you mean, Father," said the son. He buttoned his shirt against the cold as night slithered closer. "And then the ocean tries to take something back from humans, is that right, Father?"

"Yes, you are clever, my son," the father smiled, his eyes flashing. "If you're afraid after the fishing incident, Nature has actually already opened your mind. Nature is the mother and father of humanity. If the ocean says, 'Give back my coral,' human beings must stop taking it."

"Can the ocean talk, Father?"

"Yes. The wind carries the waves to the beach. They come talking and singing together."

For a few minutes there was silence. Someone was playing a flute.

"Who plays the bamboo flute on a night like this?" the son muttered to himself. The quiet resumed; only their soft breathing could be heard.

"Father, will you tell me a story?" the son asked hopefully.

"A story about what?" The father smiled as he looked at his son.

"I want to hear a story about our village, a story about Tenganan Pegringsingan," answered the son.

"My son, for years you have asked me to tell you that story. Now the time is right for me to tell you. If I cannot finish it this night, I will continue another night."

The son's face lit up.

"Listen carefully now . . ." the father began.

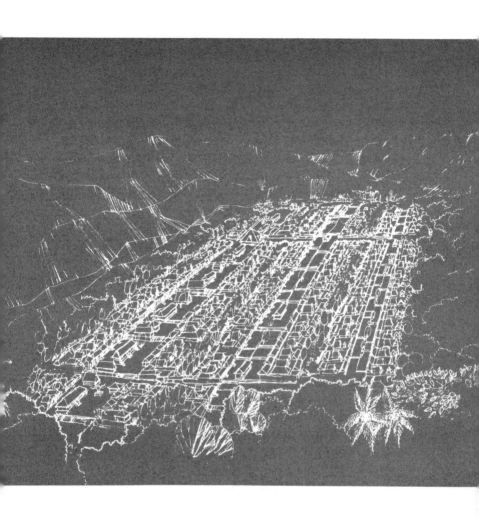

THE ORIGIN OF
TENGANAN VILLAGE

The Arrival of the Bali Aga

In the 8th Century A.D., in the village of Damalung, nestled in the foothills of the Dieng Mountains of Central Java, a yogi, Rsi Markandya, meditated. Then he left the Dieng Mountains and went to stay on Raung Mountain in East Java.

During his meditation at Raung Mountain, the Great Rsi received spiritual signs. One night, he saw a flash of light in the east. A mountain chain was lit from west to east. Far in the east, he saw the peak of Mount Agung, reaching like a ladder to the sky.

A few minutes later, the light disappeared and a wind storm began, with drizzling rain. The lightning flashes called to each other as they whipped the earth. Not long

after, he heard a magical voice booming from the sky. The area lit by the flashes of light, from mountain top to mountain top, would become his.

Rsi Markandya was very happy. He told the news to the mountain people of Aga village. They were industrious and successful farmers, and had become even more prosperous when Rsi Markandya had moved there. He always gave them useful advice and they had adopted him as their leader. Rsi Markandya's news was interesting to them. They asked the Great Rsi to lead their journey to the new land.

One day, 800 people, led by Rsi Markandya, started out from Raung Mountain and headed east to Bali Island. When they arrived on Bali, they made a clearing in the jungle. Some of the villagers died of disease or of attacks by wild animals.

Rsi Markandya was very sad and returned to Raung Mountain to meditate and ask the gods to grant his wishes. On his return to Bali, he was accompanied by 400 followers from Aga village. So now there were 1200 people from Aga. They brought seeds and equipment—provisions for the new village.

After clearing the jungle, they created a place named Sarwada (now called Taro, Tegalalang). Rsi established the Gunung Raung temple there and also the Gunung Lebah temple in Ubud and the Besakih temple at the foot of Mount Agung, which became the mother temple of Bali.

The original residents of Bali from Aga village, Raung Mountain, are now called Bali Aga.

Some settled in Bedahulu and, later, experienced the incident of the loss of the horned horse.

The Loss of the Horned Horse

1

In the 10th Century A.D., the Pengastulan temple, in the capital of the kingdom of Swa Prabhu in Bedahulu, had been busy for weeks.

There was going to be a big festival there. The king was to present offerings to God, and make a sacrifice in thanks for his kingship. The name of this king was Betara Dalem Dharma Udayana Warmadewa. The ceremony was named Aswamedayajnya.

A thousand people came from all over the kingdom to prepare for the ceremony. The palace was decorated very beautifully. The streets were made clean and the house fronts were adorned with dangling **penjors.** In Pengastulan temple, a special collection of umbrellas and banners was set up.

In the daytime, these protected the people from the sting of the sun. The red, yellow, blue, and white cotton of the umbrellas was decorated with gold paint, symbolising the glitter of lightning.

The edges of the umbrellas were decorated with a cotton fringe border, the green and red tassels representing the procession of the King's followers.

Some villages donated bamboo, others firewood, chickens, fruit, and more than a hundred pigs. The animals were slaughtered and cooked with vegetables, coconut and sauce to make **lawar.**

The most important aspect of the ceremony was the sacrifice of the King's favorite horse. The horse was strong and quick and could run like the wind.

He often led the King into battle, hunting in the jungle, or to see the countryside.

His body was white but his tail was black. He was one of a kind in Bali; there were no others like him.

This horse had horns like a cow. When he ran, he looked like a white cloud splitting the sky and sounded like the swoosh of an arrow.

His name was Uccai Srawa, and he shared his name with the horse who sprang from the holy Amarta waters, when God stirred up the Mandaragiri Mountain at the beginning of the Era of Man.

The King felt sorrow at the sacrifice of his horse but the ceremony demanded it; only a special animal could be sacrificed.

The gamelan orchestra played all day and night making the treetops tremble with enjoyment.

The wind carried the music to the mountaintops and to the middle of the ocean, where waves as large as mountains became small as a baby's hands.

The people were waiting in the streets for the King's procession to pass. In the palace, the King sat on his throne, borne by soldiers. The Queen, Sri Guna Priya

Dharmapatmi, followed on her throne with her children.

Uccai Srawa was decorated with a glittering costume. His crown was made of the young, yellow leaves of the coconut tree. He walked gently, slowly, to the sound of gamelan music.

The procession started out from the village and followed the decorated route to Pengastulan temple. The people joined the procession and the line grew long.

The horse himself seemed to understand that he was to be sacrificed. Tears flowed from his eyes.

His body sometimes trembled, his tail always swinging, and from time to time he panted. He was proud to be the sacrifice for the Aswamedayajnya ceremony. But to separate from the King was very hard.

The procession continued. Hundreds of people followed behind, carrying offerings on their heads.

Some people brought umbrellas, banners, long flags, and sacred weapons. The horse led the procession. His bridle was made of white cotton rolled long, and held by two soldiers.

As the procession approached the temple gates, the priest came out to welcome the King. Suddenly the horse did not want to move anymore. He became quiet and stood tall. His ears straightened up. From his horns came a blue-white smoke.

The King's heart throbbed. He really knew the character of his horse. Many people tried to pull the horse by his reins. He remained still. They tried to push him.

Suddenly he neighed and reared up on his hind legs. The people were stunned. They tried to still the horse but he kicked and thrashed.

Uccai Srawa became wild, his eyes like fire. His ears stood up; his breathing became hard. The people crowded around and the horse crushed some of them and ran through the procession.

Many people tried to stop him, but they were flung back by his attacks. No one could catch him.

He ran along the road until he was hidden in the twisting path. Many people chased him.

Finally, following the King's orders, the people entered the temple, prayed, and then went back to the village.

King Udayana was saddened by the disappearance of Uccai Srawa. He paced up and down in the palace. The priests and officials sat before him.

Those who had chased the horse returned, unsuccessful.

"My people," the King said, "What has happened could not be avoided. I know Uccai Srawa was angry with me. He thought I betrayed our relationship. Therefore, starting tomorrow morning, search for that horse until you catch him. Don't return without him. I will replace him with another offering."

The people nodded. They could feel the King's sorrow over his favorite horse.

"And remember, don't ever hurt him," the King continued. The people nodded again. The palace was quiet.

"For the man who catches the horse, I have a reward. This reward is so special its value cannot be expressed by money."

That night, the Minister gathered the people who would search. He divided them into groups covering the north, south, east and west of Bali Island. Ten trustworthy servants of the King were assigned to the east; they prepared to hunt the horse that night. That group was known as Peneges.

The next morning the groups started out from the kingdom. The Peneges group headed south, and then turned east, toward Gianyar, Klungkung and further east. At the same time the Bratan family went north towards Singaraja.

2

There is a white sand beach and there is coral. The waves never stop rolling there. The night before, the sea rose high.

Some coconuts, half eaten by squirrels were left on the beach. Some of them had been tossed by the waves, and thrown back to the beach.

The coconut trees grow in rows, their leaves swaying in the wind. Beneath them the tongues of the waves hiss and crackle.

Not far from the beach there were green hills and some bald and brown hills joined in a horseshoe shape, surrounding a low plain. To the south were two islands obscured by mist: Nusa Penida and Nusa Lembongan.

Ten people were resting on the beach. They wore **krises** tucked into their **selendangs**. In their hands they held spears decorated with tassels. Nearby their horses were untied and grazing.

Some of the people got up and entered the sea with their spears. Some sat by the water's edge and put their legs in. Others went in as far as their shoulders and returned with fish as big as their arms.

"I caught one," someone said. "Let's make a fire and cook it."

Some of the men gathered around, wanting to see. Others collected dry grass and dry coconut fiber. They put their **krises** aside.

They made a fire by rubbing dry sticks together between their hands on a bed of arenga palm fiber. Soon the fiber smoked. They blew the smoking pile and it was ignited.

The smell of the roasting fish set their stomachs rumbling. More fish were caught, skewered, and added to the fire.

The men talked loudly while eating, laughing and satisfying the hunger of the past few days.

"We almost died in Klungkung yesterday," a slightly chubby man said, laughing. "When we entered the village, people were afraid. They ran away."

"They sounded the **kulkul.** We didn't know where they came from—they just surrounded us."

"I saw Bendesa's face go pale." The speaker's odd laugh rang high.

"But we are ten people with weapons. Why was Bendesa afraid?

"I wasn't afraid," the man called Bendesa answered. "But when sharpened weapons surround us, and I'm in the front, my heart shrinks."

"A shrunken heart is fear."

"I wasn't afraid, but my horse was. He is not used to battle," he said in self defense.

"If Ngijeng had not been quick to explain to them, it would have been death." The stocky man wiped his brow.

"Of course," a tall, long-faced man added, "If we're opposed by a larger force, we will fall."

"How did it begin? What provoked their attack?" someone asked.

"It was Prajurit. Just as they had found the tracks of Uccai Srawa, daylight ended." A tall, broad man spoke. "He was annoyed and needed something to do."

"So what did he do?"

"A dog from the village ran by and he followed chase on his horse, throwing stones at it," the larger man continued.

"The dog continued to run, Prajurit following and yelling, until they reached the village."

"The noise of the dog attracted more dogs."

"And then?"

"The people came out, prepared to meet a band of thieves."

"How suspicious they were when they saw our horses and weapons!" The man sat back and sighed.

"Forgive me. I was so let down when darkness came. All day without food, only coconut water. And you gave me the duty of climbing for the fruit." It was Prajurit who spoke.

"You became annoyed, you say?" the huskiest man asked.

"Yes, when I saw that skinny mutt look at me, it set me off. It was skinny, but so damn loud!"

"When the villagers realized we were the King's delegates, they even gave us food!" The chubby man was laughing.

"It won't happen again," Prajurit's voice was flat.

The last two who had been fishing returned, their **sarongs** and long hair drenched. They hauled in the biggest catch of the day. The fish flapped; the men were exhausted.

"We almost lost it," they gasped.

"The *tenggiri* fish was brought by the waves to the beach. If he hadn't been caught by the coral, we would never have got him."

"I speared him, but he slipped away. So I threw my **sarong** around him and he was trapped."

"We have fish enough for tomorrow's journey." It was the chubby man again.

"Whooo! This fish has tried my skill." The man holding the fish in his wet **sarong** laughed deeply, exposing a hole where his front teeth should be. "My eyes are burning with salt."

The others clucked in astonishment. They were full of admiration for him.

"How about our journey?" the toothless man asked. "Shall we go on, or return home?"

"It's better we go home," said Bendesa, his face clouded.

"We haven't seen Uccai Srawa yet. No one we've met has seen him!"

"If I may, I think we should continue as far as the eastern shore," Prajurit offered, "Who knows, the horse may be there!"

Prajurit pointed east. The sun was already high over their heads. "It's all for nothing if we return to the kingdom now!"

"If we lose this challenge," the stocky man rubbed his feet, "we may lose our heads."

The men nodded slowly.

"That is right, friend. We're all with you. We'll all succeed or fail together!" Prajurit swung his **kris** in the air. "From the start we had a pact. We don't return without that horse!"

"Right!" the chubby man added. "No return without success. Let's begin quickly!" He stood and the others got to their feet.

"Where are we going?" asked Bendesa.

"Onward," the answer was emphatic.

"Yes . . . but where are we going?" Bendesa insisted.

"Which way do you think best?" The chubby one was confused. There was no agreement among them.

"We'll follow the beach east," said Prajurit. "It's the natural course."

"I disagree," the chubby man spoke again. He had

another idea. "We must look in the foothills. That land calls us. It could be that it called Uccai Srawa too. It's difficult for him to climb too high. If he's there, he'll be easy to spot."

"Yes, yes." Bendesa thumped the man's shoulders. "Uccai Srawa will be easy to spot, flashing white in the sun, like lightning, ya."

The toothless man agreed too, "But don't be in such a hurry. Let me eat my fish!"

He picked the bones from the fish and tossed a big chunk into his mouth. He continued to speak while chewing.

"For the moment, let the horse rest longer. It's a pity to spur ourselves on every day without stopping."

The men gave in easily. They settled down to rest and some slept.

Not long afterwards the dust flew as they headed north towards the bamboo forest.

Their horses whinnied and called to each other; the riders moved in rhythm, balancing their weight on their horses. They rode away from the beach now known as Candi Dasa.

Beyond the bamboo forest they came to a sword grass plain, scattered with cactus, surrounded by low hills. They decided to split up for the search.

Three hours later they met again on the plain. Only Bendesa was not among them. They waited a long time, but he had not returned. Their hearts grew tight and quickened. Each envisioned an accident, some trouble.

The forest skirting the hills was full of animals unafraid of man. There were snakes and tigers, too many to count.

"Well," Prajurit broke the silence, "We must look for Bendesa."

"Let's wait a while," the chubby one suggested. "A little longer and the sun will sink."

"If we don't pursue him now, we'll have to do it in the dark. The forest is too dangerous!" the husky man exclaimed.

"What do you think, Ngijen?" The chubby man put the question to him.

"Hmmmm, someone must climb a high tree. Our sight is obscured by this grass," Ngijen said, brushing aside some of the grass that blocked their path.

Ngijen was known as the clever and wise one among them. He was adept with a spear and often invited to join the hunt with the King. When he aimed his spear, his prey rarely escaped. His spear had eyes.

Prajurit was pleased with Ngijen. He jumped on the back of his horse. He rode to the highest tree and climbed it.

Far away he could see a small black point moving closer. Bendesa! He reported back to the group.

Soon they heard yelling and galloping. The nine men mounted their horses and broke away. They carried their spears, prepared for the worst.

The rider and the yelling came closer. His breath rose and fell hard. His face was flushed.

"What happened, Bendesa?" They all began at once.

Bendesa's horse bucked. Ngijen rode close and grabbed the reins, bringing the horse to a stop.

"There is ... there ..." Bendesa's breath was labored. He pointed north.

"What happened, what happened?" the chubby man spoke softly. He offered him water in a bamboo cup. Bendesa continued to gesture madly toward the north.

"Th ... th ... th ... there was something there."

"What happened Bendesa? What has frightened

you?" The bamboo cup was still held out to him.

"There, he's still there."

"He? Who?" they asked impatiently.

"Uccai Srawa."

"Ah?!" they gasped.

"Yes, Uccai Srawa, there!"

"Uccai Srawa?!" they yelled together.

Bendesa finally took the cup from the chubby man. He drank in long gulps. His breathing was still hard.

"Are you sure you saw him?" the toothless one was incredulous.

"Sure, I saw him. I found his tracks and they led me to him on the northeast side of the hill."

"Why didn't you bring him here?" the stocky one waited for an answer.

"He ... he ..."

"He what ...?" several broke in.

"The ... the ... that horse." Bendesa stopped suddenly. He was nervous.

"The horse ran?" Prajurit asked.

"The horse is dead."

"Dead?"

"Yes, he's dead!"

"Come on, let's go there!"

Without waiting for an answer, Prajurit kicked his horse to start and all followed to the northeast side of the hill.

When they reached the place shown by Bendesa, they saw the white horse with the black tail lying stiffly on the ground. His nose was bloody, and one horn was broken.

They dismounted and felt the corpse for signs of the cause of his death. It had only small scratches and was still warm.

"This horse died by himself," the toothless man said.

"Nobody killed him."

"I think so," the chubby one's brow furrowed. "These scratches are from trees."

"Still a little bit warm. Maybe he died a couple of hours ago." Ngijen said.

"How did he die?" asked Bendesa.

"Looking at the blood on his nose I'd say he was very tired," the stocky man offered, "And he may have just dropped."

"The mightiest of horses, who can run like the wind, how could this happen?"

Bendesa exhaled through his teeth. He couldn't believe that Uccai Srawa could die.

"He was searching for his own death," Ngijen said. "He didn't want to be sacrificed for Aswamedayajnya ceremony."

It was nearly dark. They continued talking about Uccai Srawa. The following day they had to report to the King.

"Only two people can report," said Ngijen. "It should be Prajurit and you, Batuguling." Ngijen pointed at the two men. The chubby man, whose name actually was Batuguling, nodded his head.

"Somebody wait here with me, we'll guard the corpse from wild animals and robbers." All agreed.

That night the men alternated watch; the roar of the King of the forest made the guards more attentive.

They burned sword grass around their camp.

The night passed without incident. The tiger was kept at bay by the fires.

Later when the roosters began to crow and the sun became bright, Batuguling and Prajurit started off for Bedahulu to report their findings.

3

In Swaprabu, Bedahulu Kingdom, King Udayana and his court conferred with the hunters.

"Is it true that you found the horse on the east side of the Island?"

"Yes, that's correct. We found him dead," answered Prajurit.

"What was the cause of his death?" the King asked.

"In my opinion, he died of exhaustion," the chubby one put forward.

"There's no question of slaughter, or poison, by a snake perhaps?"

"No question, your Highness."

"There were no significant marks on the body. There was blood only from the nose," said Prajurit.

"When do you suppose the horse died?"

"A couple of hours before we arrived. The corpse was still warm."

"All right," the King addressed the Minister. "Go soon to the place where the corpse is, and take the soldiers to verify it. If all is right, I will then award these men the land where Uccai Srawa lies. The boundaries will be marked by the scent of his corpse. If all is not right, behead them all, the ten of them, in that spot."

The Minister nodded and headed off with the soldiers and the two men.

Soon after they left, King Udayana was deep in thought. His favorite horse had been found, but he lived no longer. He vowed in his heart to continue to pay respect to Uccai Srawa.

4

In the low plains surrounded by hills, the Minister stood surrounded by a group of men. Their horses rested nearby.

"Friends of Peneges," he began, "what you claim has been confirmed, and as the King has dictated, this land where we stand is now yours."

The ten men from Peneges whispered among themselves, and then asked, "Didn't the King say the land as far as the scent of the corpse?"

"Yes, he said that."

"All right, we will now dismember the corpse and the scent will travel far."

The Minister was taken aback by the wit of the men. He did not expect such a demand. But the King's word, as final as the spit that escapes the lips, cannot be retrieved.

The men began chopping the corpse, and spreading the limbs.

They placed the penis in the north, at a spot which later became famous as the holy place, Kakidukun.

The stomach and intestines they placed in the hills of the north, later known as Batu Talikik.

The head and the hair also went to the north hills, to Rambut Pule.

The legs went to the west, Papuhan hill to Penambalan.

The spot where the horse died was christened Batu Jaran.

They purified these, and commemorated them for eternity with megalithic rocks.

Over the next few days, the corpse sent its odor far, expanding the borders of the gift-land as far as the eye could see.

Unbeknownst to the King's men, the Peneges people had slipped a bit of the corpse into the clothes of the soldiers, so the scent followed them everywhere.

The King's men were astonished by the distance the scent travelled, but when they considered it was Uccai Srawa, a spiritual horse, it seemed possible. A few days later, they returned to the kingdom.

Months later, the Peneges group brought their families to settle in what is now called Tenganan, from Ngetengahang, which means middle of the low plains, surrounded by hills.

As dictated by their oath, the Peneges clan lived

peacefully with each other; even to this day they marry only within their group, and abide by traditional laws.

The Beratan clan who had been searching the north side of the Island were afraid to return to the kingdom without the horse. So they remained in the Singaraja area, establishing the village of Beratan.

"That, my son, is the story of Bali Aga and Tenganan village. The name Pegringsingan was given to Tenganan because that is where the **double ikat gringsing sarong** is made." The old man took a deep breath. His chest had expanded with the telling of the story.

"How about another story, Father?" the son implored.

"We don't have time for the telling now. Soon it will be morning. It's better if we rest. When the sun rises we will gather fruit in the forest." The voice of the old man faltered.

"Many mangoes have fallen from the trees, and the law of this village says we cannot take the fruit which still hangs."

"Why, Father?"

"We must wait until nature presents its gifts to us," he said as he rose and re-fastened his **sarong** which had loosened a bit.

The son followed suit, and soon they heard the "krosok" of a coconut falling down from a nearby tree.

The two were soon fast asleep in their wooden bed. Beside them the kerosene lamp still burned, its flame swaying as if it were dancing the secret dance of the night. The flame became smaller and smaller, little by little, and finally died. The oil was finished.

T hose were my observations from behind the bamboo wall.

My puddle has already been absorbed by the land. I enter the crust of the earth, and there I meet the spirits of many of my friends. Together we go to the stomach of the earth.

In the magma we converge and speak of many things. The atmosphere is similar to that of the conference of journalists at the United Nations—active! What we are speaking of is of no importance to human beings: it is off the record. Let that be our secret.

The next morning I go to the home of the father and son. They are not in. Their place is actually in Tenganan Pegringsingan.

There are many buffalo wondering there. A few people are inscribing sacred **lontar** texts. There are some old women weaving the beautiful double **ikat** cloth.

The homes of the people are very tidy. The land is held in common and belongs to all of the people. The village has an old, artistic heritage.

I look for the father and son in the forest of the eastern hills. I see them collecting fallen mangoes and singing. I'm content to see them and return to Candi Dasa. I float among the hilltops, following the road.

I see some children playing with pinwheels in the peanut grove. Their parents are planting nearby.

The old people laugh while they work. Sweat pours

out of them; their muscles are firm. They are full of happiness as they dig in the earth and plant their seeds.

They plant with hope and idealism; they plant the seeds of their dreams. Nature will nourish their roots and swell their buds. She will sweeten the seeds to the farmer's taste.

Before midday I arrive in Candi Dasa and head straight to the beach. There are many tourists without clothes, despite the signs forbidding nudity. Who is at fault?

I look carefully at the beach eroded by the sea. The sea eats the land bit by bit, as if it were dry bread. Coral, the protectress of the land, crumbles in weakness, almost killed by the lime makers. The ocean seems merciless. The owners of the homestays try to block her ferocity with sea walls.

I leave Candi Dasa beach and all her tourists. A few moments later I pass Balina, Sanur, and Kuta beaches. They're all the same! The beaches are all being eaten, little by little.

Whoosh . . .! I fly to Lovina Beach following the north shore of Bali. I am relieved because here the sea loves the beach. She doesn't take, but adds more to the land year by year. I feel that she takes from the south and gives to the north.

With every circuit of the island, I pass one cursed building which from above, seems to be an aircraft carrier. One question nags me: why is this big ship on land?

Many times I check to make sure it is not a soap box. It is actually the Bali Beach Hotel. Even now I am not sure what it is for.

The sun begins to set violet in the west sky. Clouds pass as quickly as time. The farmers have returned home; the big monkeys at Sangeh forest gather at the top of the trees; the small ones hide in holes. The night animals begin searching for prey. The night people begin their day.

Whoosh . . . at lightning speed I fly back to Tenganan. I perch in the roof of the father and son's home, waiting for night.

As before, I peek in from behind the bamboo wall and listen to their story. The father sits on a bamboo chair, his son near him.

"I'll tell you another part of the story, about the beginning of Tenganan village."

The son nodded eagerly and leaned closer to listen . . .

At the beginning of the 11th century, Rabu, Keliwon Wara Pahang Madu Raksa, 1001 years after Christ, Mpu Kuturan, the Buddhist priest, came to Bali. He was also known as Betara Kuturan. He stayed at Silayukti, Padangbai. He was asked to come to Bali by the King Udayana and his Queen, who reigned from 988–1001.

It was hoped that he could quell the battles and make peace among the various Bali Aga sects of Hinduism. The majority of the people were of the Indra sect. The others followed Bayu, Khala, Brahma, Visnu and Syambhu.

Kuturan succeeded in unifying the sects into the Tri Murti, or essential Balinese religion, recognizing Brahma, Visnu and Shiva. He established the Kayangan Tiga temple system, and the Desa Adat.

For this, the people of Tenganan had great respect for Kuturan. They wanted to present him with a gift of **ikat** in Padangbai. They started out from Candi Dasa in a fishing boat, but they were hit by a storm at sea, and the boat sank.

Later, as a memorial to this incident, the people of Tenganan placed a large rock, shaped like a boat's mast (Batu Manggar) in Candi Dasa.

At times too, strange and violent things have happened in Tenganan.

One day, in 1841 AD, there suddenly appeared rolling clouds of smoke at Puseh temple.

A huge fire destroyed the temple and spread to the **balé agung,** burning everything in its path. Most of the homes in Tenganan were destroyed. The sacred village writings, preserved on **lontar** palm leaf books, were lost in the fire.

The people said, *"Puhun tan ana,* (without cause),*"* the fire began and that it was the will of God. Soon after, the village was rebuilt.

In 1970, *gejor,* an earthquake destroyed the entire village and again the people built it up.

"These, my son, are the things which have happened to our village," said the father in finishing.

"Don't you have just one more story, father?"

"Yes ... at midnight, exactly, I will tell you that story."

As I listen from behind the wall, I am filled with awe. I feel the mystery of Tenganan will be opened to me tonight. I feel grateful for the opportunity to hear this story.

Listen, the father begins!

AMOK!

1

The Night is the king of the earth when the great Day comes down from the throne. The Night himself is closest to the sun.

It is the Night which gives a blanket to the island. He feeds on Bali with his darkness. He pursues the moon so that she hides in another part of the world. Dark and dark.

Who is the Night, that he is so cruel? Who is so powerful that he can make the darkness? Who is it, that climbs up and up making the dark darker? It is the great Time?

Time does not answer. He is following the journey of the great Night. So the omnipotent Night can do all.

Creeping Night changes the air, to cool and fresh.

He closes the pores of the leaves so they are not touched by the dew.

The leaves are crying; they are weak with thirst. Their faces are downcast, wilting, and falling to the ground.

The grasshoppers perch on the leaves, weary and anxious. The anteater is quiet, rolled up in himself.

The dogs of Tenganan hill howl and with sharp movements of their eyes they look at the moonless night. Every time they howl, they flick their tails and scratch the dry earth of the hill and raise dust. Their snouts are straight and their sharp teeth can be seen.

The hills echo the long howls; the sounds repeat themselves many times.

The dogs from across the hill answer with their howls. "Hauuuk hauuuuk!" Then all is quiet.

Again the voice is heard. "Hauuuk huuuk!"

Under the night without love, a man runs up the hill. His breathing is heavy; his sweat falls with a sound like a river. His body gives off a sour smell!

Dry branches litter the ground; they crackle under his step; sometimes he falls, stands up and starts again. He doesn't heed the screams of nature; he runs straight through.

Suddenly, porcupines block his path; their needles stand on end, armed and prepared. When the man approaches, they surround him. When he is trapped, the porcupine soldiers wave their needles like swords. They want to strike the sour smell away.

The man's body is attacked and completely cut up by the flying needles. He lets out a long scream. Blood runs from his collapsing body. He falls to the ground, crying in agony. His face is pitch black.

He stumbles to his feet and raises his head to the sky. He asks the great Darkness to help him.

With a loud scream he jumps over the porcupines in his way. The great Darkness laughs. His son, the man, is saved from attack.

The man continues on, falling and starting again. The sour scent of his body now mixes with blood, and makes the great Darkness thirsty.

The Darkness sucks all the love from the heart of the man with bad smell, exhausting it completely. The rank odor stays, inseparable from the man, like guilt from wrongdoing. He reaches the top of the hill.

2

In Gumung village the atmosphere is the same. Night makes the face of the world dark.

In a house lit by a coconut-oil lamp, someone is restless. The light is dim. There are no chairs or tables, but baskets holding goods hang from the beams. Their color has faded to an earthy brown.

A man paces; the hair on the back of his neck rises when he hears the howl of the dogs on the hill. The night is hot.

He breathes quickly, sits on the floor, stands and walks again, back and forth, back and forth.

His wife waits, lying on the bed, becoming restless. She cannot close her eyes. It seems the night is stalking, waiting to spring if they sleep.

"Ni, Ni, the howling drives me mad," the man spoke as he paced. "This night is so dark."

"I feel it too, Belih," she said from the bed. "The goddess looks angry, she has sent the night to punish nature."

"The dogs deliver bad news. Who has such deep grief?" The man's voice was deep. He walked to the door, opened it, and went outside. The woman got up quickly and rushed after him.

"Where are you going?"

"Nowhere, Ni. I just want to check things here," he answered. They heard a night owl from the top of a jackfruit tree; monkeys screamed in the forest.

"Oh Belih," she spoke softly. The outside air was hot too. The wind was too tired to work. She took her husband's hand and pulled him gently. Together they entered the house.

The cry of a neighbor's baby could be heard. The night must be whispering to him, frightening him. He struggled in his mother's arms.

"He feels the same as we do, Belih," his wife said as she secured the crossbar. "I hope nothing happens to us," she said twice.

"Yes, nothing," he answered hopefully.

They spoke as they lay on the bed, to dispel their unease.

Not long after, the rancid odor stung their noses, then disappeared. The husband's brow wrinkled. The wife moved closer and held her husband tightly. Fear attacked them. The smell returned, stronger this time.

The husband rose. His face was tense. The wife rose too.

"What are you going to do?" she asked.

"Shhh, quiet!" he whispered with his finger at his lips. He sniffed to find out where the sour odor came from. He took the **kris** down from the bamboo wall and unsheathed it.

"What is it, Belih?" she wondered.

"Don't worry," he spoke confidently. "Nothing has happened. I'm just preparing in case something does. The *selan bukit* snake can't enter here."

"Is it a *selan bukit* snake in the form of a man?"

"Yes. I think it's Tundung the fieldworker. He has often lost his crops to thieves. In debt and ashamed,

perhaps he has meditated and become a snake," the husband explained.

The sour smell grew. The flapping of a bat's wing broke the tense stillness of the night.

"According to the people, this snake is white with a glittering head. A sour smell precedes it."

"Isn't she the guard of Tenganan forest? Why would she be here?" The wife wanted to know more.

"The snake is the guard of the forest but sometimes she comes down to the village seeking vengeance if someone disturbs her eggs."

"What has been done against her?" The wife's question made her husband thoughtful.

"Actually I feel nothing has been done, though I've never seen her nest. But this sour smell makes me wonder if she's come."

"If she comes . . . ?" the wife faltered.

"We are allowed to kill her; she is not permitted to enter the village. She has done wrong!"

Suddenly they heard twigs cracking. The bamboo fence in front of the house creaked under an unaccustomed weight.

The husband crouched behind the door with the **kris** in his hand; the wife stayed back. She held the handle of an axe. The rancid odor was sharp.

They heard footsteps begin and stop, snorting and

an unclear voice, "Ingajen, Ingajen ..." The voice was quiet, then began again, groaning long and deep, "Ingajen ... Ingajen! Is it you?"

The voice came again, "Ingajen ... Ingajen. If you don't open the door, I'll break it!"

There was silence for a moment and then: "I know you're in there. Open the door, the door!" The sour smell spread with the words.

"Who are you, villain? It's better if you search for another victim!" the man inside shouted.

"Open up ... or I'll break the door down!" the voice shouted.

The man inside tightened his grip on the **kris.** His wife looked pale, her breathing was irregular.

"Don't come near the door! If you touch the door this **kris** will end everything for you!" the man cried out. He knew the snake could sometimes speak like a man.

"Open your door!" the voice outside grew louder. "I can draw you out with fire!"

"You scoundrel! You scum! You bastard! Who are you?" screamed the man from inside.

"I have already killed! I've already killed them!" came the voice. The sour smell grew stronger.

"You treacherous snake! You come in the night!" the man spat out.

"You can't enter the village to search for your victims!"

"I already killed them ...! I am Ingakngik," said the voice.

"Who are you?"

"I am Ingakngik, your friend!" The couple was silenced and thought hard.

"You are not Ingakngik," said the man. "Ingakngik doesn't have a raspy voice like yours, or a sour smell. You sound like a hungry snake!"

"I am Ingakngik. Please open the door." The voice

was not as strong as before, not as desperate. It was followed by wailing.

"Believe me, I am Ingakngik! Open your door. My body is sick. Please help me . . ."

The man, Ingajen, looked doubtful. He touched the wooden crossbar, ready to open the door. His right hand held the **kris.**

Suddenly his wife tried to stop him.

"Don't open it, Belih! He is not Ingakngik!" She knocked the axe handle against the wooden bed. Her face was yellow; her mouth quivered.

Ingajen was quiet. His left hand hesitated and dropped from the bar. He shouted, "Leave, scoundrel! Go away!"

"I am Ingakngik, your friend! I have already killed them!" the voice calling itself Ingakngik howled.

"Who? Who did you kill?" he cried. Only the howl of the dogs could be heard.

"Fine, I will open the door! Stay in the yard," he said, resigned.

"Don't try to come near the house, until I know who you really are!" Ingajen opened the door. The bad smell enveloped him. From the darkness he could see the shadow of a wavering figure. It turned to approach.

Ingajen cried out, "Stop!"

The shadow tried to stop but wavered again and crumpled forward to the ground.

Ingajen stood quietly in the doorway, his wife behind him. He suspected the shadow was tricking him.

He took the lamp which hung on the door frame in his left hand, the **kris** remained in his right. He was cautious. The shadow rolled on the ground; its odor was sharp.

Ingajen brought the lamp closer to the figure. The pool of light revealed a large, muscular body. Ingajen moved closer. The face was soiled with blood. It remained still. Was he dead?

The face was oval; the jaw strong. His nose was flat; the nostrils large. His hair was matted; there was a mole on the left cheek.

"There's no mistake," Ingajen said.

"Who is he, Belih?" the wife asked from a distance.

"Ingakngik!"

"Ingakngik?"

"That's right, he is Ingakngik. Come here." He called his wife closer. When seeing the man, the wife's mouth tightened. She could not speak. Her throat closed.

Many strange voices rang. The monkeys on the top of the hill moaned, imitating the howls of the dogs.

Ingajen carried Ingakngik into the house, took water from the kitchen, splashed him. Ingakngik's breath rose and fell heavily. His body was covered with scratches and cuts, and smelt rotten.

Ingakngik opened his eyes and began to cry. His body shook.

Ingajen's tension eased. The man thought to be an evil snake, now laid out on his floor, was his friend.

He offered water to his lips. With great difficulty Ingakngik opened his trembling mouth and gulped the water as it passed his throat.

"Be still ... be still, Ingakngik," Ingajen said and his wife echoed.

Ingakngik closed his eyes. He was unconscious. In his unconsciousness he repeated to himself, "I've gone amok; I've already killed them all."

The couple looked at each other out of the corner of their eyes. They had questions as big as Tenganan hill.

They lifted the man to the bed, washed him with warm water and made a poultice of **boreh** leaves.

The couple laid out a grass mat and bedded down for the night's duration. Their sleep was deep. The **kris** remained unsheathed beside them.

Upon awakening, Ingakngik's mind was full of questions. His body was covered in cuts and bruises and blood.

He tried to move his body but there was shooting pain and stinging everywhere. He cried out in pain.

Soon he could sit up; he still gave off a sour smell. His stomach rumbled with hunger.

He rubbed his eyes and lowered first one leg to the floor, then the other. The dim light of the coconut-oil lamp made it difficult to see.

He looked around and saw the couple sleeping soundly, the **kris** beside them catching the light.

Walking with difficulty, he bent over and picked up the **kris.** Suddenly his eyes lit up; his face became wild. The couple slept, ignorant of Ingakngik's action. He swung the **kris,** his memory returning.

In the east, the great Darkness began to surrender his territory to the great Light. Squawking chickens and wild animals heralded the triumph of the great Light. The great Darkness fled to the west.

The events he recalled made Ingakngik shiver with fear. His step unsure, he nearly fell. Leaning against a pillar for support, he tried to keep from falling.

Slowly he approached the sleeping couple. He held the **kris** ready to use. Crouching beside Ingajen, he raised the **kris** in his trembling hand. An unseen power stopped him. He was filled with doubt.

He tried again to strike the sleeping man. The **kris** was intercepted. Fear came over him.

The scream of the great Dark, struck by the Light, made Ingakngik pale. He felt weak. He walked to the door and dropped the **kris** there. He went out among the trees and was swallowed by the forest.

Ingajen's neighbor was surprised to see his door open. Last night was very hot, perhaps he slept with it open.

She peered in the door and saw the **kris** lying there, the couple unmoving on the floor, a trail of fresh blood.

"Ingajen, Ingajen," she called. They didn't respond. She cried again loudly. They remained silent. Her mind was racing.

"Ingajen, wake up!" she yelled franticly.

He was quiet. His wife stirred, yawned, then woke up. The neighbor was relieved.

"Somebody opened your door?" she asked suspiciously. The wife nodded and shook her husband. The two of them rose. Ingajen immediately searched for his **kris.**

"There it is." The neighbor pointed to the doorway.

Ingajen walked over to his **kris.** It showed no signs of violent use. He let out a sigh. Then he saw the blood on the bed.

"Where is Ngakngik?" Ingajen was anxious. He looked at his wife.

"Who is Ngakngik?" the neighbor interrupted.

Ingajen's wife was stone-like, waiting for her husband's explanation.

"Someone came in the middle of the night. He was badly cut and smelt strongly." Ingajen swallowed deeply and continued, "Ingakngik was his name."

"Where did he come from? Why did he smell bad?" the neighbor demanded.

"He is from Bungaya Village," the wife answered quickly. "He's a friend of Ingajen's."

"He said he'd run **amok,** and murdered, but I don't know where or whom," explained Ingajen.

The neighbor woman's brow furrowed as she tried to imagine what happened in the house last night.

"After we cleaned and dressed his wounds we fell asleep. We didn't know he left," the woman explained further.

The sun shone through the trees. Ingajen's chickens were demanding freedom from the pen. The hen and chicks had been quiet through the night.

That morning, the news of the incident at Ingajen's house spread through Gumung village. The peaceful village became agitated, but no one knew where Ingakngik had struck.

People gathered at Ingajen's home to hear him tell of the night's event. The story was spread far and wide by peddlers passing through Gumung.

3

Sasih Desta, the 11th month of the Tenganan Calendar, about one century ago.

In three days there would be the ceremony of Ngejot Gede, part of *Taruna Nyoman,* the coming of age ceremony for boys.

The girls must wait for the *Turun Medaha* ceremony.

For its duration, from the 8th month to the following year's 8th month, the participants of *Taruna Nyoman,* twenty 12 to 17 year old boys, slept in an ashram. In the daytime they stayed with their families.

In the *ashram,* the boys are trained to participate in society. Every night two of them have guard duty; food is sent to them from their families.

This night the group looks heroic. They wear no shirts, just *selempot* scarves, and seamless *sabuk tubuhan* belts in the black and white *gotya* pattern at the waist. They hold blowpipe weapons in their hands.

They are young; the atmosphere is light, jovial. They tease each other, and sing Balinese songs together.

One night an incident changed the happy atmosphere to one of sorrow. Tenganan became a basin of tears, an ocean of blood.

The wails could be heard everywhere. Almost half

of the village was burning, many corpses lay stiff, hacked by sharp objects. The families of the dead stood in pools of tears, unable to stop the flood of sorrow. Sadness.

After the corpses were brought to the families, there was a general meeting. Some spoke falteringly of the events; others listened.

"Last night I sat in the village yard," a man began. "Suddenly I saw the **balé agung** burning. I heard cries for help to stop the fire. I saw Ipandes walking in Pemarepan, and a black shadow jumped and brought him down."

"Iwantun came and the shadow overtook him too. I Wantun's wife cried out and she too, was ambushed in the *Balé Kancan*. She fainted."

"Because it was dark I could not recognize the shadow. It darted to the home of Iboddo just as he was coming out. The shadow stretched out his hand to the stomach of Iboddo. A moment later Iboddo dropped to the ground."

"Iremrem ran to them with a **kris.** The shadow was ready for him. Before Iremrem was aware of it, his **kris** was snatched from him and he was flung five meters, clutching his chest. He rolled to a stop on the ground."

"I turned to chase the shadow but I couldn't move. I couldn't even speak. The shadow screamed while attacking the people. Before I knew it, sixteen people became his victims. Dead." He ended his testimony.

The people were restless and tense.

"Why did it happen here in such a peaceful village? What were they guilty of that this happened to them? Are there other witnesses?" asked the one in the middle, the leader of the meeting.

An old man, his hair already white, stood up.

"I'm sure the shadow is human. He carried the **kris** which he took from Iremrem and killed him with it. I don't know how many others he stabbed with it."

"Many tried to catch him. He entered Idarni's house

and set it on fire. Isengker and I tried to stop him there; he jumped the wall and entered another house. We pursued him."

"He is a madman! Every home he entered he set aflame. He abandoned his **kris** and then carried a torch."

"When we approached him he swung it towards us. He would have set my head burning if he hadn't tripped on a rock. He lost his balance and the burning top of his torch flew over my head."

"I swung my **kris** at him but he ducked and ran north. We tried to intercept him but he jumped over a three meter wall and into Tete's yard. We cornered him there."

"Though I was empty-handed I knew I could fight him."

"He looked worried; there was no escape. On Tete's wall there are many tall cactus trees. He saw the thorns. We were prepared to fight him to the death."

"Suddenly his lips moved as if he were reciting a *mantra*. Before we could recover from our surprise he rose into the air and flew a few meters over us. We were dumbstruck; he had escaped! Actually he didn't fly over the cactus, but went out the back way to Tete's house."

"The people were making a racket, yelling madly. I too, lost my composure. The man pursued was lost to the darkness. We soon heard a splash in the buffalo waterhole. We rushed there and saw bubbles rising to the surface. The sour smell hit our faces again."

"The pool was stirred up and the man disappeared like smoke. This is all I know." The man ended his story. He was sweating profusely. The people breathed long sighs.

"So what do you think, Irenis? The man may have fallen in the waterhole?" asked someone.

"Yes! If you ask me, he fell in," answered the old man with certainty.

"And he wasn't found?" another man asked.

"We lost him," Irenis said.

"And who was the man?" the leader demanded.

The people were stone-like. Because of the darkness nobody could describe him.

The people agreed to search the pool for the body, and before sunset, to bury the victims of the man who ran **amok**. "That which comes from the earth must be returned to the earth, not burned," according to the Indra Sect of Hinduism.

The next morning the members of Tenganan village spread out to the hills, the ocean, the buffalo grounds, the rice field, but they couldn't find him. He seemed to be swallowed by the land.

The news of **amok** Ingakngik spread far. From Gumung village it continued to the valleys, rice fields, forests. Soon everyone knew. The Tenganan people met again and agreed to search further, in Bungaya village.

Under the guidance of Ikarti, thirty people were sent to verify the story. They needed proof that it was Ingakngik who ran **amok**.

The road to Bungaya was littered with volcanic rubble. It was lined with forest and passed through the hills. Monkeys, pigs, porcupines, and anteaters ran clear of the approaching footsteps of the messengers.

The lullaby sound of the forest gave way to the rhythm of war. The Tenganan group reached the east side of the hills, descended to the valley and crossed the river. The river also questioned their presence. Her voice became stronger.

The stones turned their sharp sides down to allow the men easy passage. Nature did all she could to help solve the problems of Tenganan village.

4

In Bungaya village, the family of Ingakngik was saddened. Ingakngik had changed so drastically. His body was full of needles and pus and smelled bad.

Ingakngik locked himself in his room and wouldn't talk. Sometimes he screamed and would cry madly.

His family heard the news of his **amok,** but they were unable to believe it. It's possible, they thought, that some enemy started the stories.

Ingakngik, who once enjoyed laughing and joking, now looked like a monster: weeping and wailing and smelling bad.

"Do you know anything about the change in your young brother?" the father asked his son. "Why is he like this?"

"How could I know, Father? He won't speak to me."

Certainly his behavior hadn't been strange until now. Why suddenly the change?

The father sighed deeply. Until now this family has been stable, harmonious.

"Does he have enemies?" His father tried to uncover the mystery.

"I don't think so; he had many friends, everywhere. In Bugbug, Bungaya, Kestala. I cannot count his friends," explained the brother. "So why would he have enemies?"

"A young man so handsome, that he drives the girls crazy, running **amok**—impossible!"

"I don't believe it either, Father, it's just chickens squawking," the brother said and drank his glass of water.

"Ah! I can't believe Deva has sent this incident to punish us." They were mute. "Try to call Ingakngik!" ordered his father.

"He will not come, Father! he is so sick that a small movement makes him cry in pain. Yet when we give him medicine he throws it far away," explained the brother.

"He must be pushed to drink **jamu!** Massage his body with **boreh** leaves. If he isn't forced, he will be a long time recovering."

"Yes it's true, Father, but ... when the people see his eyes and hear his screams they are afraid to go closer."

The wind blew gently; a gecko was heard on the roof. The cows outside mooed lazily, the feed half-eaten. They seemed to know that something had happened.

The mother of Ingakngik was preparing lunch. She wiped away tears with the end of her **sarong.** The family ate together quietly, their thoughts moving everywhere.

5

The messengers from Tenganan led by Ikarti entered Bungaya village. The people of Bungaya became tense; they whispered and tried to predict what would happen.

Someone ran ahead to Ingakngik's home to tell of the arrival of the group. Many followed the messengers; their faces looked expectant. They did not know who they should support if a fight were to break out.

The dogs barked loudly as the thirty men passed. The dust rose around them on the main road. They turned into the lane and passed the house gates. The family was waiting. They stood like a wall in front of the house: the father in the doorway, other men on the steps. There were dozens of the people in Ingakngik's family. It was the largest in the village.

They carried **krises** in their waist-scarves, their spears leaning against the house wall. They were prepared for anything.

"Today, my friends, we seek Ingakngik," Ikarti began.

"I am his father!" the man said shortly.

"Waa, this is lucky. We have a matter to bring up with you." Ikarti spoke softly; his face was wise.

"Tell me what you want!" the father said gruffly, his voice trembling. He eyed the messengers without turning his head.

The villagers assembled behind the Tenganan men. They were ready to join when the fighting began.

"May I enter your house, friend?" Ikarti bowed respectfully and straightened up.

All the people looked up at Ingakngik's father. His lips were drawn tight, downturned, arrogant.

"No, you cannot enter!" he said suddenly.

"We are from Tenganan!"

"We don't care where you come from!"

"We only want to see him."

"Impossible! He is very sick!" His father tried to control his anger and fingered the **kris** at his waist.

"If we use force?" Ikarti said threateningly.

"There will be more victims!"

Ikarti's brow furrowed; his face was like bronze in the sun.

"In other words, you acknowledge that it was Ingakngik who ran **amok** in our village?!"

"I didn't say that! That's your conclusion!"

"We have the right to search!"

"You can't decide what is right from one side only! You have no right to judge us!" the father said in defense.

"Doesn't he have the sour smell?" Ikarti fished for the answer.

"That's our concern. Sour or not sour, it's the business of this family!"

"So . . ."

"Don't try to intimidate me! You will never enter this house!" The father put his hand to his **kris.** The family members did the same. The Tenganan group was quiet; they didn't move; their eyes were attentive.

"What if we report to the King of Karangasem?" Ikarti seemed to be stretching time.

"That's your right! That's your problem! But you

have no right to enter this house, over my dead body!"
The father's voice rose.

Unbeknownst to him, one of the messengers separated from the group and slipped into the Pandan trees,
behind the adjoining house.

He crouched forward, mumbled something and
suddenly leapt over the wall separating the houses. He
somersaulted a few times in the air and landed on the roof
of Ingakngik's house.

The sour smell arose from a different house. He
jumped south to it, seven meters, and perched on it like
a bird. He made an opening in the coconut leaf roof. The
bad smell stung his nose. He peeped in the room, saw a
man covered in running sores, lying in the bed. The man
moaned low and muttered **"Amok, amok!"** to himself.

After making sure it was Ingakngik, the messenger
leapt back to the first house. He walked down to the lane,
turned left and rejoined his group.

His absence went unnoticed by Ingakngik's family.
It would have been easy for him to kill Ingakngik, but that
is not the right way. Things must be done the right way,
however difficult.

The messengers whispered among themselves.
Suddenly they turned and left without a word. They
passed the Bungaya village gates. The village people

breathed a sigh of relief though they were still full of questions.

The Tenganan group was swallowed by the curve of the road, the tassels of their spears blown by the wind, trembling, searching for the right way.

Ingajen and his wife gave their testimony about the night that Ingakngik had visited them. The neighbor woman too, told of finding their door ajar in the morning, the trail of blood and the **kris** lying on the floor. These were the witnesses who could condemn Ingakngik.

Was it Ingakngik, or could it have been another man? Was it possible Ingakngik ran **amok** but in another village, not Tenganan? The questions pursued the walking man.

The sharp stones along the road stabbed his feet, but he paid them no heed. He thought of nothing, only proof.

The right way required proof, nothing more, nothing less.

The man hurried along the road, pursuing the messengers of Tenganan. When he passed others on the road,

he asked them which direction the group went. He ran the way they pointed.

After passing the river, he turned left and followed the zigzag course of the road. From far away he saw the group of thirty men walking as one.

"Stooooooooop!" he yelled over the distance.

The messengers stopped, astonished that someone had followed them. They readied their **krises**, prepared for anyone trying to block their way.

"Stop, stop! I want to talk," he panted as he reached the group.

"Who are you?!" asked one of the messengers.

"I am Ingajen, from Gumung Village. I am a friend of Ingakngik!" When they heard the name of Ingakngik, the men grabbed their spears. Ingajen fell, his body trembling. Dozens of spearpoints were inches from his body.

"Be still, friends!" the leader said to his group. "We need to talk to this man. Put down your spears. Don't intimidate him."

The men lowered their spears, but they remained cautious, alert at all times.

"Speak!" Ikarti said abruptly.

"That night, Ingakngik came to my house after running **amok**," Ingajen mumbled haltingly.

"Speak more clearly!"

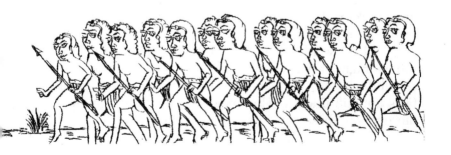

"I want to follow along to Karangasem to give my testimony."

The messengers were surprised, but very suspicious.

"Throw your weapons down!" Ikarti ordered Ingajen.

"I am ... I don't carry a weapon ..." Ingajen said in answer.

A man checked his body and found nothing. Their trust of the man grew.

Ingajen told of the incident of that night. The **amok** event began to unfold. After stopping in the forest, the group continued on to Karangasem, one more man in their fold.

6

Jero Kelodan, the Minister of Karangasem Kingdom nodded. Sometimes his brow wrinkled.

The problem was difficult and he had been ordered by the King to solve it. A heavy burden was on his shoulders; if he couldn't solve it fairly there would be trouble between Bungaya and Tenganan villages.

Sixteen people were dead as a result of the **amok.** A high loss! There had never been an incident of **amok** in that area.

There was enough strong evidence to convict Ingakngik of the crime, but he didn't want to hurry. He wanted the problem to be clear first.

The law of the Tenganan people held respect for others high; it was not jungle law. The Minister was concluding, "My brothers, the incident did occur but the facts are still unclear. The evidence points to Ingakngik, but give me three days' time to give you my verdict. I, as representative of the King, am grateful to you for your help and wisdom!"

The messengers nodded. They were happy knowing the problem would be finished in three days. They returned to Tenganan village.

The Minister sent his officers around the kingdom to investigate other incidents of **amok.** There were none. They also checked for other buffalo watering pools, but there was only one near Tenganan.

They guessed Ingakngik got the sour smell when he fell in it. They gathered the reports from Pesedahan village and Ingajen. It sounded bad for Ingakngik!

But was it really he who ran **amok?** The Minister was confused; he stroked his moustache. Sometimes he scratched his head. The price of justice is expensive!

One testimony remained unheard, that of Ingakngik! If he pleaded guilty, all would be clear.

The Minister Jero Kelodan sent a message to the family of Ingakngik. With that letter, the secret would be opened! Ingakngik must meet justice in Karangsem Kingdom!

7

After reading the letter from the Minister, Ingakngik's father paled. He felt sweaty, hot and cold. His hands shook. His body was like cotton in water. He must turn in the son who laughed only a few days before, and now cried in pain.

"Ahhh misery, who can we trust?" Never a problem in his life until now.

He remembered his son as a child—a plump, healthy

baby with soft skin, kicking his legs when feeding at his mother's breast, laughing at his father's gestures near his face. He felt deep happiness.

The baby's eyes were black, a little blue, then changed to deep brown with black rims.

His teeth began to grow from the front to the back of his mouth. When learning to walk he tottered and fell, getting up again.

His father recalled when his baby became a little boy. After the tooth-filing ceremony, he became a gentleman, handsome. He gave him a beautiful **kris** and patted his son's shoulders proudly: I am Ingakngik's father!

Once his son spoke to him about his girlfriend in Pesedahan village. Had their relationship ended?

His mind returned to the **amok** in Tenganan village. Ahhhh, idiots! He believed in his son more than in the talk of others.

"I must ask Ingakngik himself, now!" The father stood and walked to his son's room. His stride was strong; his face looked straight ahead.

"Don't . . .!"

The soft voice he had known many years stopped him.

"Why not?!"

"He is really in pain." The woman's voice moved him. The voice he'd known so long could melt his hardness. But not this time. Ingakngik's father's action was from his heart. He made a move again.

"Belih . . ."

"This problem must be ended now."

"He's sick . . ." She didn't continue; she began to cry. The creased skin at the corners of her eyes was witness to her son's life's journey.

She sobbed, her husband held her in his arms. She hid her face in his chest.

"My wife, my wife . . ." he whispered. "You are the

most noble woman in the world. You are the woman who has been my friend through happiness and sadness. Why has our fate . . . turned this way? . . ." The man began to sob. He stroked her hair, which was waist-length, black, glittering like her heart.

"Oh, come, let's sit, my wife." The man led his wife to their house. In the corner of the house behind the wall, the brothers and sisters of Ingakngik were also crying.

Later that afternoon, the family held a ceremony in the home of Ingakngik, to ask for guidance with their problem.

The bell of the priest was like a net holding them. They could see the lighted path which was very narrow.

The confession of Ingakngik was the key. All believed he was honest. If he said he was guilty, he was. If not, he wasn't. The right way must override; this was the principle of the family.

At the ceremony, Ingakngik was required to confess his actions. All the members of the family prayed. The smoke from the incense rose, made trails, then disappeared. Ingakngik wore white from head to toe.

The moon had not yet appeared; the night began to smile. The night, source of the **amok** incident, would hide his secrets no longer. The wind quickly changed direction from East to West, then flowed from North to South.

Suddenly small holes opened in the ground and flying white termites emerged. Few at first, then many, as the praying inside continued. Yet the day before there was no rain. Why did the termites leave their kingdom??!

The temple yard was filled with the flying insects. Though five lamps were lit, the yard became dark. The insects sought out the lamps, blocking the light, and burning themselves to death. Many lay on the ground. Others crashed in the air, falling wingless and running.

The frogs came soon, feeding on the corpses. The strong termites dragged the others back to the holes; they didn't want them to be eaten. Those still alive rose up, running here and there madly.

They founded a new territory, the males following the females closely. The white termite incident, out of season, stirred the hearts of the family.

"What kind of sign is this?" they asked in their hearts.

Tomorrow their choice must be given to the King. If the family sides with the son they will be destroyed. If they give him over to Justice they will grieve.

Certainly, if he's brought to Karangasem, he will be sentenced to die. The father was confused by his dilemma: to hand him over or not. Only the testimony of Ingakngik could solve the problem. If he says he isn't the guilty party, they must support him—against everyone, even the King himself.

Ingakngik was sick with the wound of the buried secret in his heart. Fear overwhelmed him. After the ceremony he was carried to the cemetery by his father, brothers and uncles.

Their steps were uneven. They walked as if unseen hands pulled them in opposing directions: first, urged towards the cemetery near the temple which held Shiva's throne; then, urged home, away from the horror of it all.

The moss on the broken wall of the temple seemed to render it sacred. Many young banyan tree shoots grew along it. The roots came out in places and tried to reach the land. Many insects hid among them.

Behind the *Pura Dalem* temple stood a group of bamboo trees. When the wind blew, they brushed each other and rustled longingly.

The group stopped at the cemetery. Their hearts contracted and pounded as they waited for the time.

"Speak," the father shattered the silence. No one answered.

"Speak Ingakngik, please speak!" his father urged.

He remained quiet. His fear rose again.

"Let us hear your testimony. We are your family!" he spoke haltingly. He didn't want to ask.

Ingakngik didn't speak. A tear fell on his cheek. He wiped it away with the back of his hand. He sobbed. His legs shook. The four sighed together. They averted their eyes from him, all except his father.

"My son, make your heart strong. Give us your story. Clear things up." Ingakngik stopped crying. He looked up for a moment, then down. His lips were held together tightly. He wanted to die with the secret.

"Ingakngik!!!" his father exhaled, resigned. "Tell your story, give your testimony to Shiva Deva!!"

When he heard the name of Shiva Deva, Ingakngik's face changed. His body straightened up and his chest swelled.

"All right!" Ingakngik said. "For Shiva Deva I will speak!" He was quiet a moment, then swallowed hard. The others were attentive, awaiting the words of Ingakngik.

"This is how it began," Ingakngik started his testimony.

8

"In Pesedahan village there was a *Gambuh* dance performance. Though the night was moonless, I really wanted to go to the performance. I know many beautiful girls in Pesedahan. There is one girl in particular who catches my fancy. I wanted to meet her.

"That night I dressed carefully. As an afterthought, I took the **kris.** I laugh when I think of it now. I paraded around my room, smiling at myself. What a fool!

"I looked at the **kris** my father gave me at the tooth-filing ceremony. It paled beside the special clothes I was wearing. I wanted a more beautiful one!

"There was one kept in the family temple. It was a sacred one, handed down in the family. It had a wooden handle inlaid with gold. The sheath was made of *cendana* wood, and gave off a warm smell. The metalwork was excellent and was etched with fingerprint markings.

"People would look up when they saw me carry it.

"I crept to the family temple. I knew my father would be unforgiving if he knew I used it. I noticed my father slept immediately after the sunset. It was unusual for him. He often sat outside at that time, enjoying the evening's coolness. My mother sat outside that night, making *Mejejahitan* offerings.

"I entered the temple and went straight to the **sanggah,** where the **kris** was kept. I opened the door; it creaked. My heart beat loudly. A strong wind blew across my face. My hands groped in the dark, then held the **kris,** trembling.

"I lifted it, and found it heavy. I felt weak and dropped it. Ahhhh ... why was I so shaky? I rubbed my hand; I felt cold and almost gave up, but remembered how proud I would feel wearing that **kris.**

"I heard somebody close the door of the house. I

jumped. Then there was silence. I was sure my parents were sleeping.

"The calm from the hills of Tenganan stilled my trembling. Slowly I reached for it again. This time it felt lighter. It was only my fear which made it so heavy before.

"I tucked it in my waist-scarf. I scaled the wall and left the house. I did not want to be seen!

"On the road I was ill at ease. I felt I was being followed. I looked over my shoulder, but there was nothing there. The voice of the night animals made the hair on the back of my neck stand up. I began to worry. When I arrived at Pesedahan village, the *Gambuh* dance had already begun.

"I elbowed my way through the crowd. Wooooo! The dancers were very beautiful; their costumes glittered. They danced while singing.

"Suddenly my body was trembling, long and deep! My eyes grew large and unblinking. I was out of control. Members of the audience fell as I pushed my way through the crowd. I had no volition of my own. I was propelled by something I could not see. I could not stop it.

"The people began to panic. The dancers and musicians stopped. Everybody surrounded me and tried to catch me. My power increased. If I brushed someone aside, they were flung away.

"My hand was drawn to my **kris** and became stuck there. I could not draw it, though I could not pull my hand away.

"The people were screaming wildly. I leapt suddenly like a cricket, over the crowd and ran away.

"They tried unsuccessfully to catch me. I was moving very fast, towards the forest where I stopped. I panted and collapsed. I felt weak.

"A few minutes later I regained consciousness and wanted to go home and talk to my father. I knew he would be angry, but it would be better to tell him. I shuddered to think of what would happen if he heard it from someone else first. I walked halfway to Katimaha temple and my body stiffened.

"Something unseen pulled me in another direction. I had no power over it. It continued to drag me. Suddenly I heard soft whispering, 'Well, Ingakngik, why do you try to stop **amok?** Come back and **amok** in Tenganan village!' the voice beckoned again.

"I covered my ears with my hands. Oddly enough, I could hear it even more clearly like that. My body continued to walk in the direction I didn't want to go.

"When I entered Tenganan village, my hand held the **kris.** Suddenly I wanted to see fire. I quickly started one and set the **balé agung** aflame. It looked beautiful burning. I shouted with joy.

"I was shouting for people to put out the fire, but when they came, the **kris** in my hand speared them. I was in trance!

"I don't know how many were victims of my **kris.**

I went from house to house, setting them on fire.

"Two beings, whom I thought were supernatural, chased me. I leapt over a three meter wall. The spirits followed. When I tried to enter the house, they stopped and cornered me. There was no escape.

"On the north wall were *blatung* cactus, their needles sharp. I had dropped the **kris,** I don't know where. Without it, I felt I had some control over myself, but my strength had been exhausted. I tried to shove the beings away, but I was afraid.

"I recited the *mantra* as taught by my father, and became one with the earth and sky. I stamped the ground three times and felt re-energized.

"I was free from the pull of gravity. I flew over their heads, and followed the path of the wind out the back door.

"I did not know about the buffalo watering hole and fell into that sour, stinking pool. People were still chasing me. I managed to climb out of the pool and ran to my friend's house in Gumung village. I then understood the spiritual nature of the **kris.** I was not strong enough to carry it.

"This is what happened to me, Father. Against my will, the night of **amok**," Ingakngik ended his story. The weight on his heart lifted; his chest opened.

His father took a deep breath. The hearts of the others beat hard.

"I must die, father. I am ready to pay for my wrongdoings," he said flatly, resigned to greet death.

His father was thoughtful, his heart cut in two.

He heard the confession of his son before him, but did not know what he must do: stand behind him or give him over to the authorities?

"Where is the **kris** now, Ingakngik?"

"I don't know, father. I really don't know. After it had its fill of blood, it returned to the earth!"

"Of course. It has returned to our ancestors," the uncle sighed.

"The **kris** has returned to the earth, we cannot follow it!" The father's brow crinkled; his voice was full of disappointment. The world felt dark.

The people of Tenganan and Pesedahan villages and the King of Karangasem would make demands on him. He was saddened. What about justice? What was the value of the law, which he had always held so highly?! He felt doubtful. His eyes closed and he dropped his head and cried. The brother and uncles were quiet, though their hearts were turbulent.

"Father, punish me ..." Ingakngik repeated his request.

"No, my son. I cannot punish you," his father spoke softly.

"Father, uncles, brother, there is only one solution. I must die! In one night I have murdered sixteen people. My guilt cannot be calculated! I must pay with my death!"

"No, it is not possible, my son!"

"What is the difference, if I die now, or tomorrow morning in Karangasem? Death ... just the same ... death will come, I cannot change that. To postpone it would torture me longer."

"I don't want to be absolved of my guilt. Didn't you teach me father, to be responsible for all my actions??!" His words fell like a river emptying into an ocean. All were quiet.

"The dead of Tenganan will haunt me, their last sighs like bees buzzing around my head, their bodies cringing and twisting when struck by the **kris**."

"Stop, my son! Do not repeat it. I can't bear it!" The strong man cried before his family. The man who had always won in battle, now lost against reality.

"Father, don't hesitate! Do it! Take your **kris** from

74

your belt! I would be ashamed if they had to come and take me tomorrow morning.!

"Before they killed me, they would parade me around the town. The people would follow and mock me and spit in my face. 'Ingakngik the murderer,' they'd shout! So, kill me father!"

"No, my son . . ." he whispered through his teeth. His heart contracted in pain.

"I only want to see the moon before I die! I want nature to smile at me before I say goodbye to her."

The stones in the cemetery were mute, frozen cold. The crickets and grasshoppers, usually singing in the night, were silent.

Suddenly, "Caw Caw Caw! Gaoooh Gaoooh Gaoooh!" Black crows perched in the top of the coconut trees, crowing.

"Father, they are already waiting for me!" Ingakngik raised his eyes to the tree tops. A crow flapped its wings; it seemed angry.

"They are the messengers of the Goddess Death. They are from *Betara Yama!*" Ingakngik's face went cold. His time was almost up. His brother sobbed quietly. The uncles lowered their heads sadly.

"Alright . . . There is only one alternative. You know that to kill you would torture me all my life." The father of Ingakngik took his **kris** in his right hand.

"This **kris** was paired with the one you used in Tenganan. Bring it to Karangasem Kingdom; ask the Minister, Jero Kelodan to kill you with it. Let it absolve you of the guilt of the first **kris.** I cannot kill you. You are my blood and my flesh."

Hearing this, Ingakngik was silenced. A pair of crows became restless and flew above the trees, squawking. Suddenly the moon appeared. All of the men looked up to her.

Quietly, Ingakngik recited a *mantra.* He joined the powers of Dark and Light. And . . . Craaach . . . Blarrrrrrrr!! Lightning struck the top of the coconut trees; everyone jumped. At the same time Ingakngik lurched forward and threw himself on the **kris** in his father's hand.

The force sent the two flying, hugging each other. The brother of Ingakngik and the uncles were stunned; it happened so quickly.

They ran to the bodies, still joined on the ground, rolling. They came to a stop and were separated by their family. The **kris** had run through the chest of Ingakngik. The father's breathing was slight; he was unconscious.

The coconut trees had burned to the ground. The squawking crows were gone. Ingakngik died the death to which he had sentenced himself. It was all over. The relatives carried the father and son back to Bungaya village.

A procession of clouds closed the face of the moon in order to protect her from the sight of her child taken by Fate.

The house of Ingakngik was quiet. The faces of those there were grey. Ingakngik's father had regained consciousness, but was lying down, weak. He was still unable to speak. His wife watched over him with a melancholy face. The family spoke of the night's events.

The morning sun climbed to the middle of the coconut tree trunks, turning them silver-white and glittering.

The soldiers of Karangasem Kingdom left the house to return to their kingdom with the news of the death.

The people of the village were relieved; the problem had ended. The rainy season had just begun.

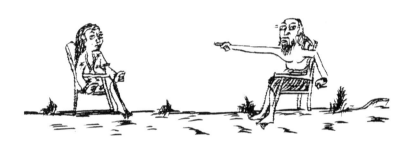

"That is, my son, the sad past, impossible to erase, because the past is history itself. But the future is still unwritten. Our hearts tremble: will the next stroke be good or bad?"

"But Father, the past has left us footprints for present." The son tried to get a response from his father.

The night wind blew fresh and cool. The voices of the frogs seemed to call the rain to the earth.

"That's right, my son, the past time has left its footprints, good and bad, sad and happy. But don't let the bad prints haunt you!"

"You must stand bravely and face your future!" The

father spoke enthusiastically. His muscles were proof of his brave past.

They did not realize the morning had arrived. The sun rolled over the east hill, and down on Tenganan village.

The moans of the buffalo joined with the squawks of hens waking their chicks. By Tenganan river, the singing bamboo and birds accompanied the sounds of boys and girls bathing.

Many children walked past, wearing white and red uniforms, ready for school.

THE PANDAN LEAF WAR

The Pandan leaf war will be held in Tenganan village in three months' time. There is plenty of time for me to see other things before that.

I roll back up to the sky following the smoke from the kitchen of a house. Up, straight up to the sky. I see the world grow smaller and smaller until it is a pingpong ball, then a small point; it disappears.

I pass many satellites made by men from the earth, Soviet, American and Indonesia's Palapa. I am surprised by man's creativity in the universe.

I continue straight up. Suddenly, all before me becomes black. I cannot see anything. It is very refreshing for me. I decide to stay there three months, returning for the Pandan leaf war.

Three months later, I leave the place above the sky, where all is black. I don't know the name of that place and I don't want to know. Whoooosh . . . !! In two minutes flat I arrive in Tenganan village, prepared to see the battle

which is staged once a year. The midday sun is just beginning its descent.

I see a long procession emerge from Banjar Pande temple. Some people are carrying long pennants and spears. A walking gamelan orchestra from Pujung Tegalla-lang plays noisily. A few people dance with **kris,** striking themselves; they are in a trance. They are free of marks or scratches.

After circling the village twice they return to Banjar Pande temple.

Soon the people gather in the grass yard before **balé agung** where they form a circle. The *Selonding* or-chestra continues to the clapping and screaming of the audience. Two judges enter the circle. The two contestants follow.

They wear **sarongs,** are shirtless and hold razor-edged, spiny pandan leaves, thirty centimeters long. In their left hands they carry circular *tameng* shields, made of woven rattan.

The gamelan orchestra plays harder. Two boys face each other, and then circle. Suddenly, one of them swings his leaf at his opponent. The crowd cries out. The boy is scratched, and bleeds. The judge stops them.

The first pair leaves the ring and two others enter. One is very big; the other is skinny and long-haired. I recognize him as the boy who receives the stories from his father.

I look among the group for his father. I see him

standing proudly in the crowd. His face is full of suspense. Someone whispers to him.

"Waaaaa, this is the first time I've seen your son in the ring."

"Mmm, he is like I was the first time in there, trembling. The second time is easy. The fight gives the boys courage. The timid become brave," said the old man.

"Why are people cowards at all?"

"Because they try to run from fear; we can't escape fear. If we face fear, we never feel it again." The man who whispered to the long-haired boy's father nodded.

They became quiet and looked towards the ring, where the boys circled each other to the rhythms of the gamelan music. I see that the long-haired boy is quaking; his movement is untidy.

The large boy circles him, jumps and swipes the smaller boy with the pandan leaf, surprising him. He successfully blocks the move with his shield. Both remain unscratched.

The small boy concentrates, his movements matching the music. His enemy is eager to attack.

At the same time, both jump and swing their blades. The long-haired boy ducks aside, striking his enemy's back. "Bhet bhet bhet." The larger boy grimaces in pain. Sweat mixes with blood, intensifying his pain.

The judge steps in. The large boy, injured and bleeding, leaves the ring.

The small boy remains in his place. A young boy is pushed into the ring. He is about 12 years old and afraid. The long-haired boy smiles at him. The younger one is emboldened.

He hops about, circling the other, swinging at him with the leaf. The long-haired boy protects himself from the repeated swipes.

He swings at the 12 year old, who puts the shield before his face, but receives the blade on his back, "Bhet bhet bhet." A second blow attaches the leaf to his skin. He recoils screaming, and cries. The people laugh.

The judge calls the fight; those who pushed him in the ring now carry him out.

The Pandan war continues, many pairs fight. The girls are flushed with pleasure, though they scream when the boys are hurt.

I leave the Pandan arena and enter the house where the boys who have fought are nursed. Their bodies are

rubbed with **boreh** poultices and they cringe at its sting, but their wounds dry quickly.

They are joking and laughing together; it looks as if they've never fought. There are no grudges held.

The father of the long-haired boy smiles admiringly; his son has experienced the Pandan battle. The young boy's mother strokes her son's head, and he no longer cries. Soon the war is over.

That evening in the **balé banjar,** there is a performance of drama-gong. The room is full of spectators. They shower smiles and laughs. Everyone is dressed beautifully.

When the drama begins, the boy and his father continue talking quietly. The Gong drama is full of drama

and suspense. It really holds the audience's attention. Drama-gong usually goes all night, ending in early morning.

At midnight I cannot see the boy beside his father. I want to say goodbye to him. My time in the world is almost finished.

I search among the people and find him huddled in a dark corner, a beautiful girl beside him. No one takes notice of them.

Do you still fish in the sea?" the girl asks him.

"Still! But beginning tomorrow, I fish in another place. There are a lot of fish there. We just scoop them up!" The long-haired boy smiled slightly.

"Really? I don't believe you."

"It's true. But only with the owner's permission."

"Where is it?"

"You want to know?"

"Yes!"

"I'll tell you, but first, you must hold my hand."

"Aduh, you!"

"Yaaa, this is good, hold tighter!"

"I'm embarrassed; people will look. It's strange, holding hands." The girl took her hand away. She smiled shyly.

"That place is far, very far, but near!"

"Tell me."

"In your ocean."

"In my ocean?"

"Yes, in the ocean of your heart, I will fish for your love."

"What's the bait?"

"My loyalty, my faithfulness."

When I look they are holding hands again. On the stage, the king and his queen also hold hands. I smile.

The morning has almost arrived. Soon I return to the sky. A star with a tail passes me. Quickly I chase it. I sit astride the tail; it is like riding a snake. We move quickly.

I continue my journey on the tail of that star. The people of the earth give it the name Halley.

I leave the world I love, the earth, Tenganan village.

I will return when my comet passes the world again, but I don't know how many years that will be. I don't know and I don't want to know!

Map of Bali

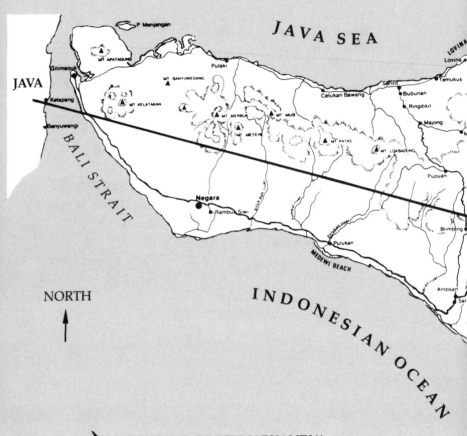

NORTH

→ THE ROUTE OF RSI MARKANDYA
IN THE 8TH CENTURY

--→ THE SEARCH FOR THE HORNED HORSE
IN THE 10TH CENTURY

Glossary

amok to go berserk, run amuck.

balé raised platform with pillars, traditionally with a thatched roof; may have walls on one or two sides; found in temples, houses and public places in villages.

balé agung large *balé* in village or palace where meetings are held.

banjar the most basic organizational unit of the Balinese village; membership is compulsory for all married males, as is attendance at monthly meetings used as forums for making village policy and resolving disputes.

boreh a mixture of roots and leaves used as a poultice.

desa adat traditional village; based on the Balinese Hindu administration system.

double ikat *ikat* means "to tie"; double *ikat* is a type of weaving found only in Tenganan village where both the warp and the weft of the cloth are knotted and dyed to make the desired patterns.

gringsing "flaming cloth" made only in Tenganan village by the double *ikat* method; said to have magical properties and the ability to protect the wearer from illness.

jamu	traditional Indonesian herbal medicine.
kris	double-edged dagger, often with a snake-like, twisted blade, said to be endowed with magical powers.
kulkul	hollow bamboo or wooden cylinder beaten with a stick as an alarm signal.
lawar	traditional Balinese food, often served at ceremonies and festivals, made of finely sliced meat, vegetables, and spices.
lontar	palm leaf manuscript; Balinese literature is traditionally inscribed upon palm leaves with a sharp instrument. Soot is then rubbed into the incisions to darken them. A *lontar* "book" can last hundreds of years.
penjor	decorated bamboo pole used in Balinese ceremonies.
prahu	small outrigger fishing boat.
sanggah	small family shrine.
sarong	cloth with the ends sewn together, worn by both men and women.
selendang	long narrow cloth, usually worn as a sash or shawl.

About Madi Kertonegoro

There is something that is very difficult for me to do—that is to write about myself. I have tried before but always unsuccessfully.

I search for a quiet place, but it is still difficult to write there. After thinking a while, I realize that the block comes from the fact that I don't like to write about myself.

To write about myself is like standing, exposed, naked before a mirror, circling, turning and smiling, laughing or crying with disappointment, at the lines of the face and body that begin to show.

Then the questions always come. "How long has this muscle been moving? How far has this leg walked? How many hundreds or thousands of times have I inhaled or exhaled?"

It's difficult to answer these questions exactly— impossible! It's easier not to think about them because once we begin to think, we will be struck by the question: "What have I done in this life?" If this question strikes me, you, he, she, us or others, it's better to just grin. Don't answer! There is no answer for that question!

For me it's a waste of time. Much better for me if we're talking about our childhood, which has many sweet memories.

I remember going with my mother to sell charcoal in the market. When we walked home she put me in the basket she used to carry the charcoal in. All the way home I would dance and sing in that basket. I covered my face and hands with ash and smeared it on my mother's face too! We were such a spectacle that people laughed at us. My mother didn't feel shame. She was laughing too.

Back at home, many neighbors gathered and encouraged me to dance like *Gatotkaca*, the "Superman" in *wayang kulit*. After each performance my mother would give me fried bananas. I wolved them down straight away. This happened many times; after dancing, eating!

Sometimes I danced with my young sister—she as Arjuna, the beautiful prince, and I, as the giant. I was always forced to lose the fight.

I asked my neighbors if I could dance the role of the good figure, so I could at last win. But they said I was much better as the evil figure because my body was as big as the *gentong* water vessel in our kitchen, and my face was long and thin like a criminal's face. Ha! ha!

My neighbors liked to tease me. Once, when I was about four years old, they told me I was not the son of my mother, but the son of a goat!

The news reached my mother's ears. She just smiled. It was different when my grandmother heard. She got very, very angry. She went to the neighbors and squawked at them. They told her why they said I was the son of a goat.

A few days earlier, my mother went to the market and I stayed home with my grandmother. She was very busy cooking, so she wasn't watching me.

Quietly, I sneaked outside to wait for my mother's return. She usually brought home fried bananas for me.

A mother goat and her kids passed by, bleating. The kids were feeding at their mother's teats right in front of me. I was so hungry waiting for my bananas. My throat felt dry. Before I knew it, I was under the body of that goat and drinking her milk!

I didn't think anyone could see me, but my neighbors came and called others. It was really amusing to witness the son of man become an animal.

I stopped drinking when I felt full, stood up and ran to the house to sleep.

Since childhood I have liked to eat. My hunger never stops. One afternoon not long after the goat incident, I saw many kinds of food and a cup of coffee on the table in the middle room of my house. I ate and ate until it was all finished.

Later, I heard the angry voice of my grandmother. The food was an offering for our ancestors.

Usually my grandmother left food in that room for three days, so that when the spirits of our family returned to the house they could enjoy it. After three days, the living members of the family were allowed to eat the food. It was bad luck to finish it after it had been on the table only one minute.

My uncle used to take me bathing in the river behind my house. It was a sacred place. One day after he washed me, he left me alone on the bank.

My hunger rose. I walked along the side of the river. Near a cave I found piles of food. Happily, I sat down to eat. My uncle was searching for me with the help of his friends. They found me hours later still enjoying the offerings in front of the cave. They brought me home.

At that time, the Ambarawa village people believed the caves, trees, mountains and seas were guarded by the devil. To appease these spirits, offerings had to be made. Even now I don't try to discover the reason why people give offerings to nature. Everybody surely knows.

The big question for me is why people must be

hungry. I am confused by this. What is the mystery inside hunger? I become more confused!

At home my family was worried that I would be cursed by the spirits because I ate their food. Evidently I wasn't. I just grew healthy and fat!

Until I was six years old, I liked walking along to the sacred places, eating the offerings I found there. The neighbors called me "Madi, son of the devil!"

In my house, like other Javanese houses, there were three rooms. The room on the right side was for the landlord, the left side for visitors and guests, and the central room for offerings. My family practiced Moslem law, but we also followed Javanese tradition, a mixture of animism, demonism, Hinduism and Buddhism.

We were not a rich family. Life was very simple, limited. There were times when it was difficult to find money to buy rice.

Even when we could buy rice, we extended it with water so it never became properly cooked rice, but porridge. This way all the family members could eat some. I hated porridge!! It made me more hungry! Maybe that's why I hunted for offerings. I needed more food!

When I was three, my father went to Sumatra to work as a farmer. He was a good farmer. In his letters to my mother, he told how he had established rice fields there. My mother remained in Ambarawa with my sister and me.

My uncle in Yogyakarta heard about the financial problems in the family, so he adopted me as his son and brought me to Yogyakarta when I was six years old. With a sad heart, I left my family and village.

In Yogyakarta, my uncle's home was very well run. All was tidy. Before sunrise, we woke up, prayed and began the housework.

I went to school, played around, and in the evening I studied the Koran in the mosque. I could no longer walk and search for offerings because in the city people seldom made offerings. Also I could eat at home until I was satisfied. My uncle's family was rich.

Sometimes I felt tortured by the strict discipline. I didn't have time to relax and be lazy.

My aunt and uncle did not like strong voices; they spoke softly. I had to move quietly without speaking. I was unhappy because I liked to listen to the radio and read history books out loud. Many times I cried because I had very few opportunities to do that—only when the family went to market.

Now I understand that the discipline was good for me. It taught me to be quiet and contemplative.

At that time I wanted to play music at home but my uncle didn't like it. He often gave me bad examples of the life of artists. If I were drawing, he would ask me if I wanted to become a beggar artist, selling paintings in the street. If I played guitar at a friend's house, he would ask me if I wanted to become a beggar, playing music in the street.

In primary school, my grades for drawing and singing were much higher than for other subjects. After secondary school and high school, I went to a vocational school to learn leather technology.

There was one subject which I really didn't like: English language! I hated it!

When it was time for English class, I would sneak out through the classroom window. My English teacher told us that English was very important because it was an international language. We would need it to read our textbooks, most of which were in English.

At the time, however, I had a different understanding of the situation. I felt that English came from another planet. I was afraid that if I learned to speak English well, I would start to behave like a Westerner, like the indecently dressed tourists I saw in the streets.

Once, my English teacher brought a real English-woman to class so we could have the chance to practice English conversation.

The Englishwoman was dressed very neatly. She looked completely different from other tourists I had seen in Yogya.

What happened? The entire class was struck dumb. We looked at her and she looked at us. We felt as if we had discovered an alien from a different world. She, doubtlessly, felt as if she had walked into a zoo.

My teacher was very embarrassed because we just stared and said nothing. Not only that, but some of the boys whispered about the shape of her legs, the shoes she wore, her long nose. Somebody whispered that she looked just like the Englishwoman in the film at the Ratih theater. There was more whispering and then laughing because, by that time, we were talking about her lips and one of my friends was saying how enjoyable it would be to kiss those sweet lips.

Finally the class was dismissed. Our teacher was furious with us, above all, with me. She thought I was the one who told everyone not to speak English to her guest. She gave me an "F" for the class.

My talent for painting and the other arts was buried under the mountain of schoolwork. My pursuit of art often bubbled but never surfaced. I was afraid if my aunt or uncle saw my artistic activities, they would try to stop me.

Often I would take a motorbike to the mountains or to isolated village, recording the scenery in my mind, meeting the people there, and speaking with them about traditions, old Javanese literature or learning magic!

In those days I seldom stayed in Yogya. Almost every week I returned to Ambarawa to meet my family. I felt free to express myself there. I had many friends and together we formed a drama group, sometimes singing and painting together.

We took turns writing scripts which we produced and staged in the *Pendopo* (public house) in the village.

My aunt and uncle never knew of these activities even though the distance from Ambarawa to Yogyakarta was only three hours by motorbike. They wanted me to become a government worker, a symbol of social status.

After finishing my studies in leather technology in 1978, I worked in a leather factory in Gresik Surabaya.

The work tortured me, even more when I saw the toll it took on the other workers. Ooooh, their poverty could not be measured. They were wrung dry, milked to exhaustion.

Every night I acted with a drama group. There were many established at that time.

I really enjoyed acting in the drama group or at poetry readings because I was free to yell and make noise and people would listen to me!

Many friends visited me in my workplace, even during work hours. Friendship was everything to me. Often I left my work to meet them in the front office, where we'd talk about drama or poetry. I wasn't responsible about my work. My boss became angry and after one month he fired me!! He gave me thirty thousand rupiah and I took this money and went to Bali.

I stayed at Pejeng village and studied painting under Dullah. He had fought in the Indonesian struggle for independence. Many times he narrowly escaped death from the Japanese and the Dutch. After Independence, he became an official painter for Indonesia's First President, Bung Karno. In Dullah, I found a new father and he felt that I was his own son.

I made many new friends in Pejeng, all learning about realistic painting.

What I learned was not how to paint, but the philosophy of art. Many people advised me to follow their ways, beginning with pencil sketching, progressing to color.

I disagreed with their methods, believing that we each have our own way. I didn't worry about them. Most didn't know the distinction between good and bad painting. That is what I learned.

My adopted parents in Yogyakarta were very angry about what I was doing. To be fired from a job is a great shame for a Javanese aristocrat. When I sent them one of my paintings from Bali, they wrote a letter asking why I studied art.

I never answered their question. I only asked them for money. Actually, they love me very much, so they sent enough money for four months.

Soon my money was finished and they didn't want to send more. Where could I find some? My friends advised me to sell my paintings in Ubud, and to bring their works along with me. I agreed!

The next morning, burdened with four large paintings, two of them my own, I set out on foot. One of my works was of rice fields, the other, the face of an old Balinese woman.

From Pejeng to Ubud, the road passing villages and rivers is about five kilometers. By the time I reached Ubud, I was out of breath.

I pushed my body from art shop to art shop inquiring about the paintings. From morning until midday I walked around; no one was interested. Damn!

I was too shy to approach tourists. My English was bad! What if they asked about prices??!!

In the afternoon I rested in front of Ubud Museum. My stomach was empty, my head circling. I began to cry. Yes, I was crying. The only thing I knew was that I would return to Java the next morning.

Soon I picked up my load again. Somebody tapped my shoulder. I turned my head. A tourist pointed at the wrapped canvases. I wanted to run but another tourist came, the wife of the first.

In English they asked me to unwrap the paintings. I shook my head. They smiled. They themselves removed the newspaper coverings and looked at the four paintings. They chose three and handed me some money. Two of my works and one of my friends' was sold.

As darkness began, I returned to Pejeng, tired but happy. After that I worked harder. My painting improved and many shops bought from me. What they liked best were portraits of old Balinese men and women and rice fields. They didn't like still life paintings.

I began to meet many people with similar ideas in Denpasar. We formed a drama group called "Teater Mentah" (Raw Theatre). The money that I earned by painting, I spent on drama. My painting benefited from this. After the performances, the paintings were much better. The performances grew stronger after I painted. You can say that I learned painting from drama, and drama from painting.

The drama group in Denpasar rehearsed weekly. We rented a hall and made all of the preparations ourselves.

When we performed many people didn't want to pay. They expected a free show. At first we didn't let them in, so they stoned the building. If they destroyed the building, that would have been expensive for us. So we let them in.

Once inside, the audience was sympathetic to our work, especially the themes, but they still didn't want to pay. Soon we understood. We were the same as they were—poor! The difference being that we wanted to be seen, and they wanted to see us!

To return to the art shops time after time to sell my

paintings soon became boring. They didn't want new kinds of work—only those which sold. You can imagine the walls of their shops, like bus windows lined with the faces of Balinese. Many friends compete to sell paintings of old men smoking hand-rolled cigarettes, and old women smiling.

When I remember those days, I feel like a cannibal, selling the heads of other humans, even if only in paint. I decided not to sell my work in art shops anymore. I want to sell works which carry a message. I want to give something to the viewer!

The result? Many people accuse me of doing political art! Others say I am crazy. Some give me thumbs up approval; others raise their fists. My paintings never sell. In one year I sell one!

I often go hungry. I am embarrassed to borrow money from neighbors. Though I know they would lend it willingly, I tie my belt tighter!

The principle for painting is not to eat, but to spread my idealism. Amidst hunger I make some good paintings, poems, stories and drama scripts. During that time I dance, read poems, stage plays and exhibit paintings in Jakarta, around Java, Bali and in Sydney.

Now my aunt and uncle are no longer angry or ashamed of me. Maybe they realize this is my life. They cannot separate me from the world of art.

Acting, dancing, painting, and writing is the skin of my life. I want to dive deeper, to know the meaning of this life. I want to follow the rhythms of nature. I don't want to be opposed to her. I don't want to cause her pain.

Maybe you will ask why I have not touched upon my love life. Isn't it more interesting than the story here? How about another time? You need the answer now?!

What if I said I was divorced with one child? What if I said I had no luck in love, always turning to blackness? Ahhhh! You can form the questions and answers yourselves.

Wahhhhh! I run off at the mouth. Didn't I say before that I don't like to talk about myself? Forgive me! Until now, I though I couldn't write about myself. Really!

And if you come to my house, don't ask again about me. It's better to speak about other things. When? When you have time!

MADI KERTONEGORO